THE SUPREME WILL

or

The danger of a premature peace

H. DUNLOP

THE SUPREME WILL

or

the danger of a premature peace

Springer-Science+Business Media, B.V.
1916

ISBN 978-94-017-6726-2 ISBN 978-94-017-6816-0 (eBook)
DOI 10.1007/978-94-017-6816-0

countries, besides another enormous amount to pay for the expenses of the war generally. The damage done in Belgium, in France and in Poland has been already estimated at £ 2.000.000.000 and another enormous sum might be required for the cost of the war. The total would then be about forty or fifty times as large as the French war indemnity of 1871. The Allies would further have to insist upon the disbanding of the German army and upon the closing of all factories of arms and ammunition and the surrender of the German fleet and the surrender of territory to France, Belgium and Russia. And until all the terms of peace were complied with, the territory of the Germanic States would be occupied by the Allied troops. This, in very broad outline, would have been done by Statesmen of the old stamp, such as Bismarck, Disraeli, Metternich. And, in our time, it could doubtless be done again.

But what would be the result? In the first place the money would have to be found. Germany was before the war, and is even at the present moment, a very wealthy country. But when peace is concluded after the invasion of German territory this will not be the case in anything like the same degree. An invasion of Germany will mean devastation on an unprecedented scale. The havoc of Belgium, the north of France and Poland will be far exceeded. For if the Germans insist upon fighting to the last man and the last horse, there will be no choice. Every town and village and factory and farm and villa will become a fortress which has to be ruined and reduced in order to be taken. So it will have to be all the way from the Rhine to Berlin and from East Prussia and Silesia to Berlin. The Allies will have to cover their flanks North and South, and it is hardly too much to say that the whole of Germany will have to become one vast battlefield, one frightful wilderness of ruined houses and factories. This is the terrible prospect, as long as Germany remains in her present frame of mind. Judging from the course of the war so far, there have been no great victories or defeats which have completely changed the possibilities of the situation. There is no reason for assuming that the rest of the war will be quite different. Progress which has been slow, will tend to become slower still. And even the first invasion of German soil across the Rhine is not likely to make more impression upon Germany's martial spirit than the invasion of Alsace-Lorraine or of Eastern Prussia has done hitherto. It is, therefore, not too bold to assume, that Germany will, even in the most favorable case, only show a dejected spirit, or the first symptoms of it, in a very gradual way. And judging from the incredibly haughty spirit of her military caste, and from the boundless fanaticism of her mob, it appears quite likely that nothing but a march upon Berlin, with all its terrors, devastation and unspeakable horror will bring the German nation to its senses. This is one possibility. It must be admitted that it will be difficult to think of anything more appalling than this prospect, which, in all the hideousness of its reality, will surpass the most afwul horrors of all previous wars, all the dreadful deeds done by man unto man in the past two thousand years, put together. We are quite ready to admit that the Allies will do their best to wage war in Germany in as humane a way as possible; we will even go so far as to assume that a *humane* war might, under a given maximum of favourable circumstances, not prove to be a *contradictio in terminis.* But who would count upon such circumstances? After all, it is not the guns, but the *men* who carry on war. And, as Marcus Antonius said to the Romans, they, *are not wood, (they) are not stones, but men, and being men,* the recollection of the atrocities in Belgium, in the North of France, not to mention Poland, *will inflame (them), it will make (them) mad.*' Already now, serious papers like the Saturday Review have uttered warnings to the effect that if the Neutral Powers continue to let the German atrocities pass by without official protest, this might be taken by the Allies to mean that the Neutrals will accept awful retribution as unavoidable, and that if the Allies visit German crimes upon German victims, no neutral Power will protest against them or assume any right to do so any more than they protect Belgium's rights. It may, indeed, be asked whether it could be reasonably expected of the allied troops, with all the unspeakable horrors of Belgium and the North of France fresh in their memories, to behave with ideal correctness, once they are in Germany, once their martial ardour is fed by the enemy's opposition, its edge sharpened by all the tricks of a desperate foe, who will stop at absolutely nothing in his fight for his fatherland, for his ideal? Even if the Allied armies commit only a small part of the German enormities, the total, extending over a very much larger territory and a population of 65 millions, may well exceed all that the boldest imagination can picture to our minds.

If, therefore, no peace is possible except one dictated to the Germanic States by the Allies at Berlin, it will be dictated to what can hardly be more than the remnants of two once prosperous monarchies. Two large countries of whose intellectual workers, of whose labouring classes, most of the best elements will have perished or will be disabled, the remaining population of which will be plunged in the utmost depths of moral and physical misery. Two large countries, whose factories are destroyed, whose sources of wealth and revenue are dried up. It may well be asked in what way such States may be expected to pay a war-indemnity, or even the annual interest on it? We may readily assume that Germany's savings have, for the last 20 years and more, been largely invested in foreign securities. But it is not known what part of these has already been exported abroad, in order to keep the available gold in the *Reichsbank* at Berlin. The fall of the value of German exchange, which amounts to about 30 percent since the war broke out, and which means a most serious depreciation of the gold-value of the Reichsmark, must have stimulated exports enormously. And since exports of merchandise and manufactured articles from the two central monarchies have dwindled to a mere shadow of their total before the war, the Allied Powers being by far their best and wealthiest customers (the exports of Germany and Austria together in 1913 to all countries amounted to £ 504,285.000, of which the Allied Powers took £ 238.675.000), it will hardly be possible for Germany to pay for her imports from and through neutral countries except in values which, in part, may consist of goods, but which for the greater part must be foreign securities, gold being jealously guarded in the Bank at Berlin. The need of gold in fact is so severely felt, that there is a movement on foot in Germany to sacrifice all golden wedding-rings and other ornaments on the altar of the fatherland. Austria, where far less foreign securities are held, Austria which, so far from being an investor, has placed large loans abroad, both Government loans and bonds of private companies, Banks etc., Austria has already been obliged to export enormous quantities of gold to Amsterdam during the war. There was, evidently, no other way for Austria to pay her coupons in Amsterdam and elsewhere. It is not possible to ascertain what other exports of gold may have taken place via other neutral countries, but that they have taken place is extremely likely. The continued war-taxes levied on Belgium, in this connection, are very significant.

A peace, dictated by the Allies at Berlin, then, will be dictated to a Union of well-nigh ruined countries. They will have to try to borrow the war-indemnity, for the greater part in London, Paris and New York. But who is to be the *deus ex machina* to plank down the stupendous sums required? Who will be the unprecedented financial genius to carry out this super-operation? The belligerents are too much engrossed in the arrangements necessary for carrying on the war, to be expected to care. The armies of Germany, in their blind fanaticism, are beyond everything. They continue their wholesale devastations, without evidently a vestige of uneasiness as to who will have to pay the bill in the end. Not later than last year many serious authors in Berlin openly discussed the question of a huge war-indemnity to be paid to Germany, of a wholesale transplantation of the populations of Belgium and France to Prussia and vice versa, of the pleasant prospect of solving the housing-problem of Berlin by a share of the indemnity, and so on. So long as the German occupation of Belgium, the North of France and Poland will last, devastation and spoliation of those territories will go on increasing the total. With regard to a war-indemnity, we may assume that disarmament would, to Germany and Austria combined, mean such an immense saving, that it would almost pay for the annual interest on a loan of between two and three milliards sterling at 3%.

But let us assume, that the financial super-operation is carried out by the financial genius which these terrible times will engender as the French revolution brought forth Napoleon. Let us assume — albeit a bold assumption — that money or credit can be found to rebuild Germany's ruined factories, capital to run her trade, to finance her transatlantic commerce; that the Allied Powers will be found ready again to open their markets for goods made in Germany, being reluctantly convinced that if they closed them against German goods ,they would ruin their debtor, and never get their coupons paid, and moreover ruin their best client over again, and so do themselves as much harm as they would do to the vanquished nations. The result would be that after some time, say a generation, or a little longer, the Germanic nations would recover. The birth-rate, after a war, invariably goes up. And even if it did not, the territories of Germania are peopled by a thrifty, hard-working, intelligent race. Again they would prosper. Again they would become wealthy. And the old desire for Power would return. The Germans of a good hundred years ago had hardly recovered from the thirty-years'war and the seven years'war when the armies of Napoleon brought Prussia to her knees in 1807.

And yet, Prussia, doubly, trebly ruined, recovered in a marvellously short time. But for her troops under Blücher the battle of Waterloo might have been far less disastrous for Napoleon's power than it was. And only half a century afterwards a united Germany reigned supreme in Europe, having overcome the two greatest military powers of Europe. A country, recovering from a succession of devastation and wholesale murder like the 30 years' war (1618—1648) which reduced her population from 18 millions to four millions; a country recovering from another devastation and another wholesale murder during the seven years'war (1756—1763), from yet another series of horrors in the days of Napoleon; which none the less reaches an unprecedented pinnacle of power and wealth in the latter half of the century that witnessed the fall of two Napoleons, such a country, in our day, will not allow even the most thorough, the most bitter defeat, to damp its spirits. And not only that. Can anybody who has not visited Germany, who has not lived amongst Germans, who has not read their daily press, who has not heard their talk, their boasting, their pride, who has not watched their mode of living, who has not noticed the very manner they wear their moustaches, conceive their fanatical admiration for their Army? Their Army, the spoiled child of a nation in arms, their Army, the tremendous weapon forged together by a succession of Hohenzollerns, men whose very thoughts were of blood and iron and power?

CHAPTER II.

GERMAN MENTALITY.

It is not as if Prussian militarism sat lightly on all Germany outside of Prussia. It was forced upon the unlucky race, willy-nilly. But gradually a virtue was made of necessity. Germany made *bonne mine à mauvais jeu,* and in the long run she became more Prussian than Frederick the Great himself. There is hardly a race in Europe, so much given to "Schwärmerei" (poetical fanaticism) as the Teutonic race of the German-speaking world. We must look a little more closely at the psychology of that race, in order to obtain a clear view of the situation. This necessitates the analysis of a few striking facts and symptoms. In this connection it appears noteworthy that Germany has for a very long time supplied the world with two categories of persons who represent her *psyche* in its inward conflict in a very striking manner. I mean those individuals, who represent the extremes of command and of obedience: princes and waiters. It is not too much to say, that wherever a new kingdom is founded, or a new restaurant is opened, Germany supplies the *personnel.* I do not quote those examples in a spirit of mockery, but to illustrate a serious endeavour to analyse the spirit of the belligerent who is generally admitted to be the aggressor, who has directly caused the present awful conflict. — The fact, as such, is so striking and stands out in such bold relief, that it cannot be otherwise than highly significant. — It means, for one thing, a conflict within the soul of the race itself. One of those conflicts, which, within the soul of the individual, and, *mutatis mutandis*, within the soul of the race itself, upsets its balance, and leads to extremes which in their turn may cause insanity. Nor is this conflict unheeded by the Germans themselves. Many people who know the faults in their own characters, which they are powerless to remedy, revert to bitter irony about themselves. In nations this often assumes the aspect of common proverbs. Now it is a striking fact, again, that in no language there are so many proverbs which deride modesty as in the language of Germany. The Hollanders, who live next door to Germany, and who are familair with its language in the same way as they are with those of France and England, seldom deride modesty, but if they wish to do so, they quote one of the German proverbs: *Bescheidenheit ist eine Zier, doch kommt man weiter ohne ihr.* (Modesty is a virtue but you get on better without it); *Bescheidenheit, Bescheidenheit, verlass mich nicht bei Tische, und mach' dass ich zu jeder Zeit das grösste Stück erwische* (Modesty, Modesty, forsake me not at table, and make me always take the biggest piece); *Nur Lumpen sind bescheiden* (Knaves only are modest). Here we have the national trait, the inclination towards obedience recognised by the patient himself and derided as in reality absurd, unworthy of a man. It is as if the soul in doing so, tried to recover its lost balance. We recognise the same trait in German comic papers, of which Simplicissimus is the most typical one. For years and years this paper, which has a tremendous circulation in Germany and Austria, has never ceased sneering at and holding up to ridicule and derision the very princes and their class who are so much adored in the Teutonic countries, and often in a way which shows extreme bitterness and often vulgarity. Even the great Kaiser himself has often been its victim, as much as the "Liebe Herrgott" ,his trusted Ally. (The latter is often pictured as a mild old man, in a smoking cap, with a long pipe).

The chief trait of the Teutonic character, which nobody who knows the Germans has failed to notice, is admitted to be that the average German is given to bow very low to his superiors as long as he is at the bottom of the social scale, but that he becomes proud and overbearing as soon as he has ascended the ladder, and positively insupportable as soon as he occupies a commanding position.

It is this trait, coupled with the native love of poetry and inclination to extravagant enthusiasm

(*Schwärmerei*) which makes Germany a fertile soil for that adoration of princes and Kings which is called *Byzantinism.*

The History of Germany and Austria, more than that of any other country in the world, is that of its many dynasties. The members of the Teutonic princely houses have never had the slightest difficulty in procuring admiring followers and retainers, for ever ready to sacrifice themselves and their entire personal interests to those of the reigning families. They have always found the mob ready to call hurrah! when addressed at meetings, where they found ample opportunity for quenching their thirst with enormous glasses of beer, or whenever the local King or magnate rode out in a fine carriage, dressed in uniform and surrounded by men on horseback with plenty of plumes and feathers and gold-lace and with all the absurd paraphernalia which feed a childish and naïve national fancy. I do not mean to denounce these national traits as altogether nefarious or objectionable. On the contrary ,I am ready to admit that an inclination to meekness and to obedience of superiors may indicate an amiable side to a national character. I am quite prepared to agree with those who see in Byzantinism many an admirable opportunity for self-sacrifice and for devotion. But for all that, self-sacrifice and personal devotion, of which there is a tremendous wealth in the soul of every human being as within the soul of Mankind itself, may find far better opportunities in quite different surroundings, and should indeed be turned into channels which lead to a higher purpose than that which is naturally confined within the aspirations of a princely house.

And when those aspirations, like those of the Hohenzollerns, appear to embrace those of immense masses of individuals; when they are, by dint of clever catch-phrases, made to represent a dynasty as the very incarnation of national greatness; when the dynasty secures the devoted services of a man like Bismarck, who whatever his failings may have been ,was a political genius of the first rank; of Bismarck, who said to the Crownprince in 1848 that he would not mind being hanged, as long as the rope served to tie his father's throne faster to the soil of the fatherland; we clearly see to what extremes Byzantinism may lead.

We have, then, in the German race those extremes of haughtiness and pride, of meekness and self-sacrifice, which must, in the long run, lead to mental confusion.

What has been the position of Germany in the past, and is it different from what it used to be?

The Germanic empires occupy a very unfavorable geographical position for war in the first place as their access to the world-seas is not free. On the North West and West England and Holland and Belgium bar the way. Austria's outlet on the Adriatic does not allow a further sweep than Gibraltar and the Suez-Canal. On the East and on the South East the Slavs make their presence and their influence felt by their ever-increasing numbers, although these far outpace their intellectual progress. The Germanic race has had to fight invasions from the East from time immemorial. It was their race, which, indeed assisted by the Poles, hemmed the tide of Turkish aggression under the walls of Vienna in 1683. It was their race which first sounded the knell of Turkish ascendency in Europe. But for the victory in 1689 the best part of the continent might have shared the fate of the Balkan States. It is the irony of History, indeed, which makes those who overcame the Turks, their Allies in our time; which makes them Ultra-Turks in Western Europe since the 4th August 1914!

The unfortunate geographical position of the Ger manic States is intimately connected with Germany's political History. Five hundred years ago the German Empire embraced not only the present States of Germany, but it possessed an immense coastline on the North Sea, for it included Holland and Belgium, and this would have made access to the Atlantic much easier. But transatlantic commerce, in those days, scarcely existed. As in antiquity, the known world, for Europeans, lay around the Mediterranean, the Baltic, the North Sea, and the Western coasts. The Empire also included Switzerland, a large part of Austria and of the Baltic provinces. But in our time the two Germanic empires combined are in reality only a remnant of what the Great Empire used to be. They do not occupy more than half its territory. They are hemmed in on all sides. Countries like Belgium and Holland and Switzerland, have weakened the position of the race, by seceding from the mother-country. Belgium and Holland, and the latter more especially, have developed separate languages and nationalities and they have become complete strangers to the old country, so that separation is complete, not only politically, but in almost every sense which could have formed a tangible tie.

And yet, though shorn of many of its best and most energetic elements, — the energy of Holland in the 16th and 17th centuries was quite phenomenal and enabled the United Provinces, with a population of barely a million and a half, to play a leading role in Europe — after the terrible ordeals of the thirty- and seven years'wars, after the Napoleonic upheavals, Germany led by Prussia, having overcome her military rivals in quick succession, became the leading power on the European continent after 1870!

There was, indeed, no disaster, no terror, no wholesale murder or devastion so appalling but Prussia's energy overcame them all. She never showed her spirit better than in adversity.

CHAPTER III.

FRENCH AND BRITISH RESPONSIBILITIES.

We should here mention Germany's predecessor in Ultra-Militarism, megalomania and lust of conquest, France. The symptoms of the French revolution, partly engendered by fear (of Austrian intervention) were those of insanity just as much as those exhibited by Germany now. The absurd cruelties of the "Terreur" find their counterpart in the Belgian and north of France atrocities. There was precisely the same desire to enforce French civilisation on Europe as Germany's desire of our time. All the symptons were the same. We need not look into the causes now. They were different in many ways. The results were the same: disastrous for Europe, for Germany and Holland in particular. France ruined Holland so completely that it took Holland nearly a hundred years to recover. England rid Europe of French ultramilitarism, at least without England's strong aid this would not have come about. Europe by herself would not have won Waterloo. But afterwards England declared herself disinterested in European affairs. Sir Robert Peel's last speech in 1850 laid down that principle which was, most unfortunately, to guide British foreign policy right through the eventful years of the Franco-German war up to 1877 when Gladstone inaugurated the view that England must go back to the time when the nations looked to her for liberty. — But before that time England, who rid Europe of French Ultra-Militarism, did not, or could not, prevent another power, Germany, to take the place of France. In this way England, by not interfering in 1870, is really responsible for the present war. She is now reversing her policy and, whether she will or no, she is now more European than Europe herself.

England, like other great nations, has not been entirely free from lust of conquest and megalomania. The Boer War proved it. But the liberal successors of Chamberlain restored the lost balance.

Is it correct to say that the British Navy is Ultra-Militarism on the sea? The British Navy is not a State within the State as in Germany the Army is. The British Navy obeys the commands of the Cabinet. The German Army has no orders to follow but those of its Chief who is an Autocrat. That Army overrides the councils of civil Government, and puts strategy over International Law. This is the direct cause of Germany's crime against Belgium, against International Law, against Europe, against the civilised world. Even Bismarck, the strong man of the 19th century, who, in autocratic Germany, held civil authority higher than the Army liked, could not prevail against the annexation of Alsace-Lorraine which he is said to have streneously opposed.

CHAPTER IV.

GERMANY AND EUROPEAN COLONISATION.

The Union of Germany in 1871, a Union of blood and iron, forged together by the warhammers of Moltke and Roon and Bismarck had, after a generation, brought an unheard-of advance in material prosperity. At the same epoch the great discoveries of the 19th century had opened unknown sources of wealth, and an altogether phenomenal industrial development over the entire globe. The Anglo-Saxons, who started colonising after Portuguese, Spaniards and at the same time as Hollanders and French, had confiscated a great part of the colonies, founded by these nations and had brought them all to a high state of prosperity. The United States and the countries of Spanish America had become markets whose magnitude far exceeded the boldest dreams of their founders. The colonial possessions of Great Britain and of Holland and France, by a combination of favorable circumstances, had become markets which absorbed stupendous quantities of the goods which were turned out by millions of yards and pounds by the factories of Europe, brought to that perfection which only the scientific discoveries and improvements of the 19th Century could have brought about. In China and Asiatic Russia huge territories with populations of hundreds of millions were opened up by material force, and by the wealth of France and England freely placed at the disposal of the European bourses. Only the possessions of Great Britain and Holland were not fenced in by tariffs; British India, Java and other possessions under the rule of those countries were as free to German commerce as to that of their own. The German merchants had but to walk in, and so they did, for generations. German business houses in those parts, played a leading role.

In the days when Germany was torn to pieces by her own quarrels which caused the thirty-years' war, Portugal, Spain, England and Holland and France had created colonial Empires which extended to all parts of the world. Those empires, built up by *their* treasure and *their* blood, were now open to the trade of Germany. Germany had not furnished the men, who, centuries before, had set out in tiny sailing ships, in quest of unknown lands, which they were to link to the white man's civilisation, which Germany aspires to lead, now that the real work has been done. Germany had not sent out the hardy colonists, who, with only the scanty resources of bygone days at their disposal, had nothing but their faith, their courage and their energy to transform into gardens, cornfields, plantations, and mining districts the wilds of Asia, America, Africa and Australia. Germany had not opened up Japan, or helped to throw open to European trade the colossal markets of the Chinese Empire. Neither had Germany been instrumental in throwing Persia, Egypt, or any other independent or semi-independent oriental country open to the trade of the West.

The work, which really meant the White Man's conquest of the world outside Europe, had been accomplished, when the new German Empire appeared on the scene. She found the world's markets ready made, furnished throughout with railways and telegraphs and with all their material resources developed as only the white race can develop them. The work had been accomplished before the "Kultur" of Prussia had had time to assert itself, to materialise in the new German Empire. Germany was not slow to take advantage of this extraordinary combination of favorable circumstances. Her thrifty and industrious population turned out whatever goods the other countries could produce, and her merchants and ships distributed them over all the markets, *which all Europe, Germany only excepted, had opened up and created.* An enormous increase in prosperity, in material wealth, and in the material standard of life was the result. Germany, in fact, had entered upon on era of commercial and political greatness which could not but recall the grandeur of the days of the Hohenstaufen Empire of 5 centuries before.

We have admired Prussia, at the head of Germany, in days of adversity. But try as we may, we cannot admire her in her prosperity.

CHAPTER V.

GERMAN BYZANTINISM AND ASPIRATIONS.

We have endeavoured to analyse the psychology of the German people. We have found what their outstanding characteristics are. And, judging from its terrific result, we find Byzantinism one of those with which we shall have now to deal.

The best way for a dynasty to keep its hold on the admiring mob is a display of power and brilliancy. To the good-natured mob it is enough to know that their King or their Emperor sometimes condescends to say some kind word to some ordinary mortal, by way of a mistake, more or less, to believe that he is the best and the most tender-hearted of men. They do not grudge him a life of ease and luxury at their expense, as long as they are allowed to see him drive, or ride out at the head of his well-dressed troops, with plenty of colour, plenty of drums and music. When he thus passes them in the street or on the square, or through a fine gate adorned with statues of other Kings and Emperors, the sight makes their dear hearts beat quicker, and tears of patriotism and love for their monarch come to their eyes. When they are home, they tell everybody that they have seen Him, the Emperor. Their love for the dynasty is as sincere as it is fanatic. Their appetite for seeing royal and military display is insatiable, and if the ambition of the dynasty is sufficiently intense, the mob is only too ready to feed the Emperor's or the King's aspirations at military glory. The monarch, always ready to stir the sincere hearts of his faithful subjects, often makes appeals to the Almighty, with a great, and well thought-out show of humility. This humility, for a man who commands large armies and great wealth, who is the sole head of the state, makes the monarch appear as a good and pious man after all. He is the fatherland, the nation as represented by this one man, and they are ready to die for him. He never ceases to remind them of the glorious deeds of their fathers, who died for his fathers after having killed as many "enemies" for them as they could. And they, heedless of the teachings of the Christ whom many of them profess to worship, admire the organised murder of battles in war, and in all sincerity they think that there is no courage greater than the courage of militarism, which drills men to march to the front to be slaughtered by the thousand, or to slaugther the "enemy", so as to forestall him. The War-Lord is careful to remind them that they are surrounded by bloodthirsty enemies on all sides, who are only waiting for an opportunity to attack them. And gradually, as Reade says, "the animal instinct of self-defence is converted into the ravenous lust of wealth and power." Here, then, we have militarism, ultramilitarism, as the dangerous result of Byzantinism.

The victories of 1866 and 1871 were so brilliant, that it is hardly surprising that they engendered megalomania in a race, so little accustomed to political greatness. The mistake of 1871 which tore two provinces from France, had never ceased to remind France of further danger from the East. This drove France and her saved milliards of francs into the arms of Russia. And so Germany was threatened, or thought herself threatened, from the East as well as from the West. Byzantinism, ultra-militarism and fear of aggression! Surely the powder-mine had but to be touched to explode! Germany could not "be safe without being dangerous."

But the question is yet more complicated. It was not enough for Germany's vain ambition to be in a position to sell ever increasing quantities of manufactured articles in the foreign markets of the world. It was not enough, that her newly acquired wealth enabled her to build cities and factories, gaudier and finer than anywhere else in the world, albeit of more than doubtful taste. It was not enough that her workmen received high wages, that emigration to foreign colonies became well-nigh superfluous, that on the contrary foreign labour had to be imported. It was not enough that her mercantile fleet increased by leaps and bounds. For still there was an almost unconscious feeling of inferiority; across the oceans lay the lands where German goods and the products of German intellect were brought by German ships. And yet those lands were foreign to the fatherland. Their language was not German. *Germany could make no moral conquests there any more than she had been able to discover or conquer the lands themselves when others carried the White Man's civilisation over the seas.*

But Germany was far too proud and too much engrossed in self-admiration to admit that if Russia became her best customer it was because Russia had opened up Siberia, the Caucasus, Turkestan; if South America provided immense markets for German goods, it was because non-Germans had, since the Middle-Ages, made Latin America what it is now; if the United States, and the British and Dutch Colonies afforded endless opportunities for German enterprise, it was because British, Dutch and French blood had been spilt there ever since the days of the Armada. What claim, then, could Germany advance for world-dominion?

Germany had produced great thinkers, great poets, great artists, she was the equal of all the rest of Europe, except in this one important respect: there was no Germany across the ocean. There were many Englands oversea, there was a rejuvenated Spain in South and Central America, France and Italy had found congenial climes for their superfluous populations in Africa, Russia could extend in Asia *ad infi-*

nitum, even Holland and Portugal had transplanted their languages and characteristics to large regions abroad, and even *they* had prospects of extensions which far exceeded those of the colonies which Germany had acquired.

It was a bitter thought for a race that recollected the sweet air of Empire in days of old. But there was a consolation: Germany possessed an asset which the others could not boast: the German Army! Let them, who know little else besides their shops and their trade, look at that wondrous product of German intellect, that miraculous organisation, which represented all that was strong, grand, noble, self-sacrificing in the soul of the great Germanic race! It was true that the terrible weight of ultra-militarism was more than human nature could bear; but pride forbade any but a smiling face. It was true that everything was kept up to concert-pitch, from the day the small boys went to school, through their turn in the Army, throughout their lives in factories and offices, from the cradle to the grave. It was true that the number of schoolboys committing suicide became appalling, that in the Austrian and German armies there were 1860 cases of suicide on a million of military men against 516 on a million civilians, and that in all countries the difference was far less. It was not by mere chance that the German treatment of insanity rose to be the best in the world. It came as a necessity. The church and its consoling influence had lost the hold which dynasty, fatherland and uniform had usurped. For Nietzsche had not taught his people in vain that they must not worship a degenerating faith in meekness and in the Brotherhood of Man, but that courage and material strength were the true and only idols worthy of the Great Soul of Germany.

But all that was nothing to Germany. She bore it all like a man, although it drove her mad. She knew and heeded it not. The Emperor William, regardless of Bismarck's advice, which pointed to limitations dictated by historical and geographical facts, was the incarnation of all the extravagant ambitions of new Germany, and it was an easy matter for him to carry the country with him in his race with England for seapower. It is superfluous to go any further in our search for the causes of the disaster which we are witnessing. They are manifold, but we believe we have touched upon the principal ones, and we believe that they are chiefly to be found in Germany and in the soul of her people. We are not concerned so much with the questions regarding French ideas of *revanche*, or with those connected with any desire on the part of England to forestall Germany's ultimate aim which was the occupation of the coast facing England, so as to attack her from that long line of vantage; we are quite prepared to admit that England formed, and was obliged to form, certain alliances so as to provide against the terrible consequences of that ultimate aim, whether that aim really existed in the minds of the majority of the Emperor's advisers or not; we do not deny that, in order to secure Russia's co-operation, England was obliged to sacrifice the interests of Persia, which she had very much at heart; for it was British influence in Teheran which had helped the young-Persians to set up a constitutional Government at the very doors of autocratic Russia. From the fact of Persia being abandoned by England to her former rival Russia; the road to India being thereby thrown open to the possible aggression of the latter Power, we are bound to conclude that the British military authorities were in possession of information regarding Germany's designs, which must have been of the most serious, of the most threatening nature. A great country like England cannot afford to give up its role as the protector of a state like Persia struggling to free itself from the embrace of its merciless neighbour, except in case of dire necessity, when the vital interests of the protector are in jeopardy. Neither are we, for our present argument, concerned in any inquiry as to aggressive designs on the part of Russia, or with the question as to whether England would have declared war if Germany had not invaded Belgium. *We are concerned with the results of an old fashioned peace,* after the financial super-operation has been concluded, and after the day when the world will have returned to its hum-drum life of peace and to its usual everyday existence, disturbed only now and then by a small colonial expedition or by some pronunciamiento in South America. We are concerned with the influence upon the world, exercised by a Germany which has been made to quaff the cup of bitter humiliation to the last drop.

CHAPTER VI.

GERMANY'S MORAL STANDARD.

If we wish to enquire into possible future developments, we are justified in considering that the war has shown us the true spirit of Germany clearer, better and more completely than anything else could have done. We knew of German Byzantinism, we knew of Ultra-Militarism, we may even have suspected megalomania and a lurking desire of conquest at the expense of the countries surrounding Germania. But we did not know, we could not know, of the extent to which Ultra-Militarism has smothered all sense of moral responsibility in the councils of Germany. In justifying her disgraceful action against Belgium, *post facto,* by charging the innocent Belgian Government with conspiring against Germany, this country shows a remarkable lack of reasoning, and indeed signs of moral insanity. Previous to the great flight of Belgians across the Dutch frontier Holland, which of all neutrals was best informed, knew a great deal more about German misbehaviour in Belgium than Potsdam could have wished. But when a million Belgians fled to Holland where the people speak practically the same Flamish language as the Belgians themselves, stories were heard which speech refuses to repeat and pen to describe, stories which made many a man feel ashamed of his very humanity.... and even truthful Clio herself may refuse to hand them down to posterity and consign them to eternal oblivion, as the walls of an asylum forget the ravings of the lunatics within them.

German enormities in Belgium and in the North of France, according to official reports dealing with sworn statements and proved facts which do not admit of any doubt, have revealed a state of mind in the German Army which we may or may not be charitable enough to call insanity; but which whether it is caused by insanity or by sheer criminal brutality, is extremely dangerous, as it vents itself in a general ferocity which stops at absolutely no cruelty to individuals and at no offense against piety or against the respect for ancient monuments, buildings or any private or public property. "Since a number of years", says Ibn el Athir, the Persian-Arab Chronicler in his report about the year 1220 "I have been wrestling with the decision, to picture the catastrophe of the Tartar invasion of the lands of Islam. It is too terrific; I would rather not do it. But now I proceed, hesitatingly.... Oh, that my mother had never borne me! Oh, that I might have died before, and been plunged into oblivion.... Numerous friends have urged me to put it on paper, and I have ever wavered, but now I see that no useful purpose would be served by silence, and therefore I declare the following; This enterprise means the narrative of the most frightful calamity and of the greatest misfortune, the like of which neither days nor nights have brought forth, and which has burst over all nations together, but over Moslems before the others; and when anybody would hold that Mankind, from the moment that Adam was created by God — praised and exalted be his hallowed Name above all — to this day had not been visited by any like trial, he would but speak the truth. For the books of History contain nothing which could approach it. Amongst the most frightful catastrophes which they describe, is that which Nebukadnezar did unto the children of Israel, when he killed them, and destroyed the Holy City of Jeruzalem. But what is Jerusalem as compared to the entire provinces devastated by these accursed ones, of which every capital was a double, a treble Jerusalem; and what were the Children of Israel as compared to the number they have killed, when the inhabitants of one single city, whom they have massacred, exceeded the Children of Israel? I believe that the nations of the world will not witness an other similar disaster, until Mankind appears before God's Holy Throne, and until this world passes away into nothingness.... Indeed, we are from God, and to Him we must return; there is no might nor power except from God, the most High." In this way the pious historian of the East described the days of Jenghiz

Khan and the Mongol massacres in Western Asia just about 700 years ago. Many a pessimist of our time would, in recent catastrophes, find a parallel of Mongol crimes. But even the most pronounced pessimist cannot deny the fact, that whereas the German atrocities are well-established facts, German public opinion is so impressed by their horror, that it stoutly denies their very possibility. Again, he would find some food for reflection in the strenuous way in which the statesmen of Germany try to whitewash themselves of all responsibility for the war. They all profess to wage a war of defence, a war which will decide their national existence itself. And he may ask himself, whether Jenghiz Khan or indeed whether any conqueror or belligerent previous to the time of Napoleon ever troubled himself to proffer any excuse to ease his conscience or to palliate the evil effect of his actions.

The war itself and the way in which Germany has waged war, then, has revealed two salient and significant facts.

The one is, that no nation, and no responsible statesman has uttered any other feelings than those of alarm, disappointment, disgust and shame for the war having broken out at all and that there is not a single belligerent Government which does not indignantly repudiate all guilt of having brought it about.

The other is, that not only the world at large, not only the other belligerents besides Germany, but Germany herself, are appalled by the German atrocities. We may, or we may not be quite certain of the sincerity of Germany's indignant denials; we may or we may not believe that German atrocities are part and parcel of a well thought-out system of "frightfulness". We have to admit, in any case, that hypocrisy is a tribute to virtue, which at all events points the way to it.

For all that, the concensus of the neutral opinion of the world points only one way, and it is this: Ultra-Militarism, as adopted by Germany, has lowered the general moral standard of the country and of its policy. Nor is this to be wondered at. You cannot, with impunity, make war, which is organised murder, the chief pre-occupation of the State, without horribly perverting even the noblest instincts of the human factor of which armies consist. You cannot, in adopting Ultra-Militarism as a creed, avoid carrying the contempt for the rights of others, the contempt for all moral laws which Mankind, from time immemorial, has known to be the priceless treasures which live in the depth of its very soul, and which all founders of world- religions have brought to the light, to unprecedented lengths.

And yet, we have seen that Germany, owing to various circumstances which we have tried to explain, looks upon her army, and has looked upon it for generations, as the finest, the noblest, the most brilliant of all national achievements, which more than counterbalances any national asset which Germany lacks in comparison to other nations. Germany looks upon her Army as a thing of moral and intellectual beauty, as an unsurpassed, and unsurpassible instrument of moral, physical, and intellectual education. We have countless assertions to prove this from her best authors and statesmen; her citizens and newspapers are never tired of repeating them. And more than all this: the German nation is so much struck with the extraordinary merit of this creation of its national genius, that it feels nothing but contempt and pity for those who do not possess it, and it often professes that German civilisation (the famous "Kultur") which has become flesh and blood in the Army, ought to be the leading influence in the world. There is quite an incredible amount of self-adoration and of pedantic self-assertion in all this. And but for these insane notions we may well doubt, whether the present war could have broken out, or, if nothing could have prevented it, whether Germany could have carried it on with unabated enthusiasm these last 18 months.

The extent to which ultra-militarism has debauched and corrupted Germany's morals, her political morals in the first place, is further proved by her outspoken desire to stir op Mohamedan religious fanaticism throughout the world in urging upon the Sultan of Turkey who, ruled by muddle-headed "Young Turks", has become Germany's helpless instrument, to proclaim "Holy War", a war which Professor Snouck Hurgronje, of Leyden, one of the greatest, if not *the* greatest of living authorities on Islam, has recently called "Holy War made in Germany". This authority has proved the innate absurdity of *this* "Holy War" and he calls it surprising that Germany which has produced so many clever orientalists, should not have known better. But apart from this, supposing for a moment that Turkey had possessed sufficient moral influence to provoke world-wide fanaticism, even in a hopelessly divided world as the unorganised Islamic world undoubtedly happens to be, the result would have been a calamity of appalling magnitude in all those countries in the East where the White Man's civilising influence has succeeded in creating order out of chaos, and where populations running into hundreds of millions might have been stirred up to the most awful excesses. I need only refer to Britain's 100.000.000 Mohamedan subjects in India, to the 20.000.000 followers of the Prophet in Central Asia, to the 35,000,000 Mohamedans in the Indian archipelago ruled by Holland. The latter Power, by this extraordinary piece of German diplomacy, which proclaims, at the same time, a very particular preoccupation in favour of seeing Holland preserve her neutrality, could not do otherwise than consider this attempt to stir up strife throughout the Mohamedan world with the utmost anxiety and suspicion. Fortunately, the European powers who hold most of the Islamic world under their sway, have ever shown the most sincere regard for the sublime faith of the

Prophet. Moreover, their enlightened rule has proved to Mohamed's followers that only Western civilisation, quite apart from any religious convictions, has been able to bring them a material prosperity which their own Governments or princes could not restore to them after the Turks had destroyed it. For wherever the Turks have, by the inscrutable ordainments of Providence, been poured out upon the unfortunate populations of ancient Persia, of Asia Minor, of Egypt, of India, they have destroyed prosperity and driven entire nations to desperation until the day when Western influence gained the upper hand. These are historic facts which it is hopeless to attempt refuting. But what do the Germans, themselves, think of the Turks? We need only insert the following quotations from one of the best German authorities on the History of the Islamic countries, Prof. Dr. A. Müller, in his famous work "*Der Islam im Morgen- und Abendlande*" (Islam in the East and in the West). Speaking of the Turks (Vol. 2 page 192 et seq.) he says: "The Arabs did not behave like angels when they sallied forth from their peninsula, on the contrary, as to the majority they consisted of scarcely anything but nomadic hordes, whose chief occupation was looting; but they have known how to create a great State, to evolve political and religious ideas, or to make them their own, for the sake of which it was worth troubling or even fighting. With the Turks we find nothing of all this. The martial instincts of this race, which we cannot fail even today to recognise, are deprived of all admixture of political insight or of the ability to maintain any political organisation before the advent of the Osmanli Turks.... It appears that only under quite unique circumstances, which, later on, must have existed on Indian and Anatolian soil, the Turks are able to arrive at a state which goes beyond riding and throat-cutting....". And what has the same author to say of the Osmanli Turks of whose political power we shall probably witness the final collapse? Scarcely anything more refreshing! Speaking of Western Asia and Egypt under Turkish rule, he says: "Of the great dominions, won by Mohamed the Conqueror and Selim: Asia Minor, Western Armenia, Mesopotomia, Syria, Arabia and Egypt, not a single one, under the sway of the thick-headed Turks whose only aim was extortion and the maintenance of outward order, has ever been able to return to any prosperity at all.... on the contrary, Anatolia, under the Seljuks a thickly populated and well-to-do land, later the cradle of the Osmanli themselves, is nearly a desert today." And so on for several more pages. Could anything be more apt to add intense bitterness and shame to Germany's stupendous tragedy than this relentless indictment of her Ally from the hand of one of the best German authors?

In denouncing Ultra-Militarism, we will not be misunderstood; for in so doing, we have no intention of denouncing the German nation. It is well, in these days of turmoil, when terrible deeds threaten to unhinge even the best balanced minds, to remember Burke's maxim: "You cannot indict a nation". If, therefore, we accuse Germany, we accuse the military caste of Prussia which is the main prop and support of imperial despotism; we deplore the distressing fact, that this clique has, by a combination of circumstances, and by the very docility of the German character, been allowed to poison the mind of a people which, as to its overwhelming majority, used to abhor violence in any shape or form, a people whose very love of home and of peaceful occupation, whose lofty patriotism, have been played upon, and abused until haughty pride, fear of attack and invasion alternately have driven it mad. When we hear of the Belgian atrocities, of the cold-blooded execution of civilians, of crimes which belong to the domain of psychopathology, we cannot escape the conclusion that central Europe has been disturbed and put on fire by a people that is suffering from acute insanity. The common soldiers, who storm positions with a fanatic courage that reminds us of the Madhi's derwishes [1]); the parents at home who drink Champagne when they hear of the death of an only son in battle; the professors who are honestly and sincerely convinced of the absolute superiority of all things German; the officers

---

[1]) "Die Infanterie war wahnsinnig" (The Infantry was mad) a German officer declared, speaking of the first great battle on the Yser river.

who declare that the life of a single German soldier is worth more than a beautiful ancient city and all its works of art; all these symptoms show us an entire nation of 65 millions of souls suffering from an acute attack of megalomania, accompanied by the unmistakable symptoms of dementia: destructiveness; inaccessibility to reason; temporary loss of natural affections; lack of moral sensibility. No permissible measure of passionate indignation at the enormities committed should allow us to lose sight of the fact, that we are witnessing the most stupendous calamity of all times, and that of all belligerents Germany in her self-deception and half-conscious despair is the most tragic figure. She has made her last and greatest bid for world-power, and she has failed. Those, who claim the honour of being civilised, and of being civilised Christians will perhaps do more justice to their own country and to themselves, when they do not allow "pity to drive out pity". When the police has arrested a madman who has murdered his neighbours, the angry mob would tear him to pieces, but the wise men of the jury defer judgment until they have examined the case in all its aspects. — That, I believe, is a worthy attitude for serious men and women, one that will never blur the clearness of their vision, so that, when the time comes, they will protect those who are innocent of crime, remembering that no man may be blamed for doing what he honestly considers his duty to his native land, which after all not he, but fate has chosen for him.

They will also recollect that in Germany too the minds of large sections of the population are enlightened and progressive, but that their voice, when becoming articulate in Liebknecht's and Ledebour's courageous indictment of Ultra-Militarism in the Reichstag was smothered by the ruling caste, which sacrifices everything to their fear of granting to the people any control of the machine of Government; and that the sane and sober Germany of the future may well come as a surprise to those who abhor her today.

Again, in denouncing Ultra-Militarism, it is far from us, to belittle the valient men who submit to military discipline and who risk their lives in fighting Germany and Austria together with the allied troops. They are sacrificing themselves in a supreme attempt to arrest the insane giant who is devastating Europe's fairest lands. They are policing Europe and this is impossible without militarism, the only antidote which civilised society can provide against the barbarous poison of Ultra-Militarism.

CHAPTER VII.

ULTRA-MILITARISM, PACIFISM, AND THE FUTURE.

Such then, are the ultimate results of Byzantinism Such is the appalling outcome of Ultra-Militarism.

The great argument in favour of *war*, put forward by authors like Prof. Steinmetz in his "*Philosophie des Krieges*" (Philosophy of War) is, that it ensures the survival of the fittest.

Evidently, such authors argue from the point of view, that it is in the nature of things, that living beings all have to bow to the natural law, which commands that only the fittest shall survive.

In the first place, we do not believe that Mankind should bow to the laws of nature. We hold, on the contrary, that he should find out what those laws are, and subjugate them to his own will and purpose. The difference between those authors and ourselves is this: *they* believe in a Supreme Being, who to all intents and purposes is an Autocrat like their own kings and emperors, and whose commands have to be obeyed without inquiry; *we* believe in a Supreme Being who is identical with the Universe, of which we, men, are a part, which is the part that has become conscious of its existence, and will, ultimately, be master of its own destiny.

Secondly, even apart from such philosophic considerations, we contend that War does *not* ensure the survival of the fittest. If men were animals, it certainly would. The stronger men would kill the weaker and this would improve the race, physically at least. But in our wars, the strong men are killed and the weak ones remain at home. Bullets and shells, moreover, kill men on the battlefield indiscriminately. It might be argued that amongst the fighters there are strong ones and weak ones, and that those who come back alive, are the strongest. This held good in olden days, but owing to our modern instruments for wholesale murder, the killing is done quite indiscriminately. Of course the stronger men will recover from wounds better than the weaker ones. But this factor would not be of sufficient value in favour of War, and would be much more than outweighed by the indiscriminate killing of the strongest men of the fighting nations.

It has often been said that War brings out the finest qualities of men, and that warring nations are more "virile" than others. I do not understand why we should require War to bring out our best qualities. We might just as well say that Plague and Earthquakes are good things, because the Plague gives doctors and nurses a chance of showing heroism, and patients a chance of showing their endurance, and because Earthquakes bring out our fine qualities of charity and of energy in rebuilding houses which have fallen into ruin. And as to "virility", we do not see why this should be shown at its best in murdering other people. We think that a good deal of virile virtue is required to build a locomotive or to run one at full speed. Men who plan and build railways or bridges require at least as much "virile" virtue as men who plan battles. Men who plough land, or who open up wild countries require quite a lot of virility. Doctors who risk their lives in laboratories, nurses who look after mad people or after patients suffering from contagious diseases require great courage. We are not at all sure that soldiers would not prefer to go to a battle than to look after a patient who has the Plague, or to explore countries where the natives are cannibals. As it is, there is such a tremendous lot of misery in the world, that, without war, Mankind will have more than sufficient opportunity for showing virility and courage for centuries to come. If we should have War to brace us up, we might just as well promote the spread of Cholera or Plague. That would come cheaper in the end, as these diseases at least do not mean much material damage, and leave no enmity behind them.

As to courage, required for War, we ask whether it is really courage in the best sense of the word, to plan a battle on the principle that you must only give battle when you are sure that you are the strongest. There is also a good deal of running away in good strategy. Is that courage? With troops who are volunteers the matter is different, I admit. Only the British troops are volunteers, at least by far the greatest part of them. Their courage is the real article. Our remarks as to War are not meant for them. Nor for the brave soldiers of France, Belgium or Russia, who in this war, are defending their wives and children against the atrocities of the Barbarians. That is true virility.

We are quite ready to admit that "conspicuous bravery in the field" is a very fine thing indeed, and that a man who has shown such bravery must be respected. But in modern strategy bravery is supplanted by mathematical calculation. Bravery is much less wanted than calculation.

As to the survival of the fittest races, we may inquire as to what has happened in the past, and as to whether fighting races have survived. It is not enough to judge by short episodes of History; we must extend our inquiry over long periods of time. If we go by the short episodes which are covered by some years, we shall find that, in the past, those nations, who attacked their neighbours first, and were better prepared for War than their neighbours, invariably subjugated them in the beginning, after having killed them by thousands and frightened them into submission. But during the process the invaders always lost immense numbers of their own men. Both invaders and invaded lost a far greater number of males than of females. The result was polygamy and to some extent the mixing of races. As the fighting was generally done by the men, we are even now still labouring under the delusion that killing other men is "virile", and feeds the "virile" qualities of a race. We should think that saving other men's lives often requires much more "virility" than firing a gun at them or getting a shell to explode a long way off. As the invaders were generally less civilised than the invaded, being necessarily of a more ferocious disposition, they borrowed the civilisation of the subject races and often became so thoroughly mixed with them that hardly a trace remained of the invaders.

This happened in India and in Persia, when those lands were overrun by the Mongols in the time of Jinghiz Khan in the 13th Century of our era and were partly devastated.

It happened in Europe in the centuries following the reign of Charlemagne, when Europe was invaded and ruined by the Normans, who destroyed, killed and devastated to their hearts' content.

It happened in Western Asia, when it was attacked and conquered by the sudden onslaught of the Arabs.

It happened in Byzantium and in Asia Minor and Egypt, when those countries were invaded by the Turks.

What, broadly speaking, was the outcome of these "militaristic" achievements? If ever War was "diplomacy carried on by other than diplomatic methods", those wars were.

The Mongols lost their empires either to native

Princes or to other invaders, and they disappeared from History altogether. The little good that is ascribed to them was done by the natives whom they enslaved for the time being.

The Normans (when they were not absorbed by the natives, as they were in Normandy), returned to Scandinavia, and for nearly a thousand years they have exercised no influence on the world.

The Arabs founded empires which were managed by the subject races whose civilisation they stole and afterwards paraded as their own, as the Arabs did with the Persians. After a few generations they disappeared as the ruling race and since then they have played no role in History any more.

The Turks killed and robbed for centuries, only to leave the conquered countries virtually in the hands of the original natives: Greeks, Egyptians, and Syrians, and to have to obey the orders of the Germans, the next invaders, or to the British, as in Egypt.

The fact is that killing and robbing are against human nature, which, from time immemorial, has abhorred murder and theft. Not from any innate "affability", but because of all animals Man was the most intelligent, and most intent on self-preservation, which was best promoted by mutual help and aid. The Moral Laws, which serve as Standards of Civilisation, do not emanate from a mysterious, awful Being, as was formerly believed. Their origin has been traced to the human brain. In our time the truth of all this is so strongly felt, that in all civilised countries there is a tendency to attribute offences against human life, especially, of course wilful murder, to insanity. To take the life of one's fellow-man, it is thought, a person must be insane. And it has indeed been scientifically proved that murderers and dangerous criminals generally are mentally inferior. Their sculls and brains show a tendency to atavism. Morally speaking, they are fossils. They represent a stage in human development to which the majority of individuals never returns.

When a nation substitutes murder and robbery, in the shape of War, for morality, when it ascribes to War all possible virtues, it is bound to go under in the struggle for existence. Already now in Germany children show an alarming deterioration of morals. They play at murder and rapine, and many little boys actually have become scoundrels. The whole nation suffers by this deterioration. As it has been in the past, so it will be now: He who uses the sword, will perish by the sword.

We must now return to our original inquiry regarding the results of an old-fashioned peace, the probable terms of which we have given in broad outline.

They would include the abolishing of the German Army and the closing the factories of War-material.

After what has been said of the spirit in which Germany regards her Army, it will be evident enough that there is no calamity that could exasperate Germania to a more desperate extent than this. Not only would every defeat, and the final disaster be solely ascribed to the overwhelming multitude of foes, but the fallen "heroes" would be more fervently worshipped than Saints in Churches. Is it possible to expect that the ideal of generations can be hauled down from its pedestal by the action of foreign invaders? It is more likely that the reverse will happen.

We have seen that in the past Germany, after a succession of the direst disasters, after devastations and massacres without number, has shown a most remarkable recuperative power. There is no reason whatever to believe that this power should have diminished. On the contrary, the colossal increase of scientific knowledge since the time of Napoleon, the unlimited resources of modern technical ways and means would tend to heal economic wounds much quicker than even our grandfathers could have conceived. After a generation when fresh millions of recruits will have reached the required age, the fatherland will rise again. We have shown that in the interests of the Allies themselves, Germany cannot be allowed to perish economically. The fallacy that the poverty of one nation can or will be of advantage to another, has, moreover, been exploded long ago. Just as a rich man can only enjoy his money from the moment he parts with it, so a wealthy nation is obliged to give of its wealth to other nations. Germany would prosper once more, and necessarily, her old longing for power would revive.

The memory of the Emperor William I would be as sacred as that of Barbarossa. If the course of events were to sweep away the dynasty now ruling, another royal house, with equally ancient, or even more ancient claims to national regard, might place itself at the head of national aspirations. We need not be at all possessed of extraordinarily imaginative powers to represent to our mind a regenerated Germany, taking under the wing of her Imperial Eagle all the German speaking nations of the present empires of Germany and Austria headed by a Wittelsbach, a Habsburg, a Coburg or some scion of any other ancient and glorious lineage. The Germans of those future days will not be oblivious of the days of old, when the "Emperor" in Europe was the Emperor of Germany, the days of Frederic Barbarossa and of his successors of the mighty Hohenstaufen dynasty, which ruled from the Baltic to the Mediterranean over a United Germany that embraced all the Teutonic races and had subjected some others. Nor will they be likely to have forgotten, the days of the Emperor William I ("Mein unvergesslicher Groszvater" — my never-to-be-forgotten grandfather as the Kaiser has never wearied of calling him). His Mausoleum and that of Bismarck will become so many Meccas whither the true believers in Germany's destiny will go to worship. In the meantime the world will have advanced, and Germany with it; perhaps Germany will have outpaced it in numbers and in wealth, we cannot say. Diplomats will in-vent patriotic phrases such as "Revenge or death", "Our future is on the battlefield", "A nation which does not pay off old debts, is unworthy of life" and so forth. And patriotic hymns will be sung by throats, constantly refreshed by copious draughts of beer, speeches will be held by well-meaning patriots to enthusiastic crowds. And the mob, as of yore, will forget the blood and the mire and the beastliness of war, the mob will only see the plumes and the feathers and the prancing horses; and, may be, the tens of thousands of aeroplanes, brought op to a perfection which we in our days can but conjecture. And science, having devised weapons, a hundred times deadlier than those of today, will make war a hundred times more destructive. The war-fury will break loose again. The other nations, who will have watched Germany with growing anxiety, will have kept pace with her armaments. England, which will have become Germany's latest acquisition in "hereditary" foes, England and her sister-States beyond the Seas, will be armed to the teeth. Massacre, destruction and devastation will again plunge Europe in oceans of blood and tears, and the White Man may well tremble for the fate of his civilisation, not in Europe alone, but in the entire world. For the war of 1964 will be a hundred times more terrible than that of 1914. Not only small countries like Belgium will be devastated, but large ones, like England, Canada, Australia, the United States of North America.

Previous to the war, all the Anglo-Saxon countries, who will have to keep pace with Germany, will have been forced to Ultra-Militarize themselves, for they will have to protect their mothers, their daughters, their wives, their houses, their *all*, against Belgium's terrible fate.

The Teuton doctrine that the interests of the individual should be entirely subservient to those of the State, could have no other effect than the obliteration of individuality. Germany has certainly amazed the world by the wonderful organization of her public services, not only in a military, but also in a financial and economic sense. But it may be asked whether it is not a significant coincidence that Germany lacks both diplomats and statesmen; a fact, which all Germany admits. After Bismarck Europe has not heard the voice of a strong individual man from Germany, excepting the Kaiser. He indeed absorbed the personality of every single man of merit in his surroundings. None but an extremely docile race would have allowed such a thing from such a man, who sent the famous Kruger telegram in 1896 but who, a few years later, refused to receive the exiled President and supplied the British war-office with a complete scheme for the overthrow of the Boer Army. None but a docile race, naturally inclined to abstract thought, could have been hypnotised by the abstract idea of "the State" as understood by Potsdam: the State in which patriotism becomes a cold system of philosophy, almost like the solution of a mathematical problem.

Although the Anglo-Saxon world possesses many characteristics which will shield it from the worst consequences of Ultra-Militarism, there is yet another feature of that institution which deserves special attention.

CHAPTER VIII.

ULTRA-MILITARISM STOPS PROGRESS.

When comparing Germany to the other civilised nations during the last century or so we find that hardly one of the great inventions of modern times originated from Germany. We beg the reader to understand, that we are referring exclusively to those inventions *which have completely changed our mode of living*, inventions which have caused such stupendous achievements as the annihilation of distance, and the like. We need but refer to the steam engine, to steamers, railways, and tramways, to gas for lighting, to the telegraph and the telephone, to the bicycle, the motorcar, the typewriter, the bioscope, to wireless telegraphy, to the flying machine. In view of this formidable list we can hardly avoid arriving at certain conclusions. We can hardly avoid looking for a connection betweed two salient facts which force themselves simultaneously on our attention. *The lack of inventive genius in Germany coincides with the time covered by ultra- militarism.* It would appear from this that apart from its extremely demoralising effects, Ultra-Militarism absorbs too much intellectual effort to leave a surplus for that mental action which creates the great discoveries and inventions that have changed the aspect of life in modern times, and which in future should bring to Mankind the complete mastery over Nature.

And as to other scientific inventions, we think the case for Germany is not much better. We have to consider Germany and Austria together as the Teutonic race, whose total number is little less than 110 millions, and far exceeds the total of England and France together.

Is Germany's record any better with regard to artistic achievements during the time of Ultra-militarism? Has she led the world in painting, in sculpture? With regard to the latter, the Siegesallee in Berlin gives an eloquent answer. And as to the former, there is no great German painter known generally outside of Germany other than Böcklin, who, however, was a Swiss. Holland with about one tenth part of the population of Germany, has, during the last 40 or 50 years, produced better painters, many of whom have obtained a worldwide reputation, than all Germania together. As to literature, we may say the same thing regarding Scandinavia and Belgium. The musical world may for many years have regarded Wagner as one of its heroes; but it is no exaggeration to say that by aid of a very clever advertising campaign, and by a good deal of snobbery his reputation may be somewhat over-estimated. Many thousands go to Bayreuth, the Mecca of Wagnerites, because it looks rather genteel to have enough time and money for that pilgrimage. Some critics declare, however, that Wagner's art is not free from coarseness and bombastic adornment, whilst the text and the intrigue of his dramas lack clearness and high inspiration. We can recommend, regarding Wagner and his works, Max Nordau's critical essays "Entartung".

We think enough has been shown to expose Ultra-Militarism as immoral, reactionary and in direct opposition to the interests of society. It is a highly significant fact that Pacifism is chiefly opposed by the Conservatives in all countries; and especially by so-called „Christians." As if it were not bad enough that the Teutonic peoples of Germany and Austria have been debauched by Ultra-Militarism. This is no exaggeration. On the 6th February 1916 a meeting was held in Berlin by the German Society for the care of children, to discuss the *terrible increase of crime amongst children.* The Berlin Court of Justice, in 1915, dealt with 2900 juvenile criminals, against 1902 cases in 1914. — Already before the war German criminality was greater than that of any other European country. But let this war bring us the one supreme consolation which it is capable of giving us: the conviction that it has meant a timely warning to the rest of the world, and to the Anglo-Saxon world in particular.

A regenerated Germany, then, will not only revert

to ultra-militarism with all the baneful results which we have endeavoured to picture, but all the rest of the world will be forced to follow her example. The United States of North America, by German immigration, may not be able to remain neutral, but may very well be forced by the majority to join Germania against Europe or England. And when the war of 1964 breaks out, the world will be one immense Germany; Western civilisation will work its own destruction and the non-fighting peoples of Asia will illustrate the sublime truth, that the meek shall inherit the earth.

But, supposing, it may be asked, that even an old-fashioned peace, recalling the days of Vienna and Frankfurt, does not bring a return to old excesses? We believe that even without Germany's ultimate return to ultra-militarism, the outlook is far from bright.

CHAPTER IX.

GERMANY DISARMED.

Let us assume, for the sake of argument, that Germania, after having been thoroughly beaten, repents of the error of her ways, abolishes her autocratic form of Government and sets up a Republic, in which her socialists play the leading role. Let us assume, that a tremendous reaction sets in, and that all Germania's dynastic fanaticism is consigned to oblivion; that Habsburgers and Hohenzollerns alike become exiles and that all titled persons will be afraid of calling themselves anything else but plain *Herr* so-and-so. Let us assume, in fact, that Germania is thoroughly democratised. Let us assume, further, that the Germanic democracy will not be a democracy according to Talleyrand who called democratic Government an Aristocracy of scoundrels; and that, so far from being bellicose, as Lord Salisbury thought democracies naturally were, the Germanic King Demos will be meekness and mildness personified. Let us go a step farther, and let us imagine that Germany would be divided into several small republics and that each would have the misfortune of having its neutrality guaranteed.

6

Let us picture to our minds her *Feldwebels* and her soldiers intent upon all the arts of peace, her generals preaching in churches, or turning out piece-goods in factories by the million yards a day, or making hundreds of thousands of those artistic clocks and flower-pots and knicknacks per week, which will delight, as of yore, as many good-natured folks devoid of any taste (and ready to have any rudiments of artistic feeling that may lurk in their souls destroyed by merely looking at them) as ever. Let us take it for granted, that Herr Krupp will be horrified at the mere suggestion of an indent on guns, that to behold a uniform, one is politely conducted to a Museum; let us, in short, try to imagine that things which appear perfectly ridiculous to us *now*, will come about and that the German tiger will have become a lamb. It would be almost too good to be true. But if it were true, it would only be good if not Germany alone assumed all the characteristics of a lamb.

Is this to be expected? Can we allow ourselves to believe that Germany of all nations alone, is capable of Byzantinism, Militarism, lust of conquest or megalomania? And that Russia, Italy, France, Belgium and England or some other nation will not be accessible to at least one of those evils, which must necessarily bring one or more of the others in its train?

Let us examine these questions somewhat exhaustively; but let us first assure the reader that we are, in the present war, neutral, and that our country has made up its mind to be left severely alone, without any presumption to any political influence beyond its colonial possessions. At the same time it is very strongly felt in our country, which gave birth to Grotius, the founder of International Law, that Holland, having been chosen as the seat of the International Court of Arbitration, has a moral duty to perform, namely the promotion of the development of International Law; the more so as, having been spared from the terrors of this war, she cannot be accused of being in any way biassed, except in so far that Pacifism has a greater hold on Public Opinion in Holland than in any other country.

We have to consider, first, the present belligerents: Russia, Servia, France, Belgium and England.

It is more than doubtful, whether either of these five nations will consider Germany's defeat as a sufficient expiation for the wrongs they have suffered at her relentless hands. On the contrary, nothing would appear more certain than that the mere recollection of their sufferings will be enough to stir up lingering rancours, which comparatively trifling events may easily turn into so many dangerous passions. We may, without going further into facts which have been and are being made widely known, by the press of every land, take it for granted that this consideration will apply to them all. But there are other, similar aspects of the question. It is to be expected that Germany, once being rid of militarism, will devote herself to the arts of peace with all the love of organisation and devotion to the State of which she is capable. We must here remark that in the preceding pages we have not had any desire to give vent to any anti-German prejudice. We have only desired to show the peculiarly nefarious influence of ultra-militarism upon the people of Germany and Austria. We, like all the world, loved the Germany of Goethe, of Schiller, of Heine, and of Beethoven, the sublime Beethoven, the gentle, the passionate aristocrat amongst men of music, the man, I would say, of the esoteric soul of music, his own soul, which he seems to pour out and to contemplate from yet a higher pinnacle; the land, too, of Bach, the pious, the deep, the fervent. We loved the old Germany, of which we were a part, which was part of us, of Europe. But we see, that Beethoven and Bach represent old Germany as much as Wagner represents the Germany of our time. We admire and we love the former, we are astounded and appalled by the latter, just as we love and admire depth and fervour and feel amazed by brilliancy and are appalled by an excess of force which becomes bad taste and empty rhetoric.

But whatever new Germany is, nobody will call her narrow, petty, shallow, wavering. Her enemies may call her cruel, relentless, barbaric,treacherous. But she is perfectly sublime in courage, in devotion, in patriotism, in self-confidence. Just as the Dutch language, the language of a contemplative, serious, homely people, abounds in diminutives, so the Germans show their character in the words they use most: *colossal, grossartig* (grand), *ueberhaupt* (generally), *riesig* (gigantic), *wunderbar* (wonderful). They make use of these words on all occasions and continually, even to indicate the most puerile notions. Yet they reveal a tendency to bigness, to *greatness* if you will, and in them Germania shows her unconscious self.

Now imagine what such a race, once rid of Ultra-Militarism, may be able to achieve. We know by irrefutable historic fact, that Germany has always been admirable in adversity. There is no reason to assume that in our time she will be different. Her industries, strengthened by the intellect set free by the abolition of the Army, will astound the world. There will positively be no end to new discoveries and inventions. She will be able to produce a multitude of things cheaper and better than others. Imagine the gigantic amount of energy and intellect, hitherto wasted on organised murder, let loose upon laboratories and factories! The set purpose, the subjection to discipline, the methodical way of doing things, all taken off the army and suddenly transferred to science and industry! There will be all the elements of unexampled prosperity and wealth. Would it be surprising if such a Germany, defenceless and rich, excited the cupidity of some other race, less gifted, but more numerous, hardier though less civilised?

Would it be surprising if the Bulgarians, in their inhospitable land, with their peasants always several generations behind the rest of Europe, would like some grapes from their neighbour's garden? And that if they did not get them, they would simply take them? I do not for a moment mean to imply that I consider the Bulgarians moreim moral than other nations. But as long as statesmen *as such* are ruled by another Moral Code than individuals, the interests of the State will take no heed of any moral whatever. Let us take yet another case. Supposing that Russia another fiftyor another hundred years hence,holding then about thrice the population of Germania, cannot find an outlet for her increasing multitudes except in a westerly direction? She finds every square mile in Germany occupied, only Canada and Australia would afford enough room; but those lands refuse admittance. That might mean war with England. Russia would walk across Germany as Germany now walks across Belgium. France, now her ally, might then be her enemy. Russia, now England's Ally, was England's bitterest opponent up to the arrangement of 1907. Up to that time Englands greatest statesmen had never left off warning their country against India's danger from the side of Russia. It is perfectly true that the situation has changed. The mere fact that India is more loyal to England than any conquered land has ever been to its master, the likelihood that India will gradually become a sister-state within the family of States that forms the British Empire, and will be quite able to defend itself, will eliminate all danger from the side of Russia. But there may be other causes of friction which we can only conjecture, and one of which we have named.

Again, a wealthy and prosperous Germania, unwilling to fight, may, if unarmed herself, get other nations to fight on her behalf. She may well have better diplomats in the 21st century than in our days. She may have large sums to lend. Who is going to deny the possibility of another Prussia rising in some other country outside Germany? Who would deny that Asia, with hundreds and hundreds of millions of people is not a land of unlimited possibilities? Or that some tribe in the African wilderness may learn Western science, and use it for aggression, by Germania's financial and intellectual aid?

A democratised, ultra-industrialised Germany may throw herself with as fanatic zeal as she applies to ultra-militarism, into social democracy. For several industrial products the socialist theory that the State should be the sole capitalist and producer may be put into practice. High protective tariffs may shield Germany from "dumping". But the State, having become one immense house of business, may throw itself into any particular lines of articles of export that will best suit it, and "dump" those on the markets of the world, by huge advertising campains, low prices and all the arts of selling goods which our time has brought to perfection. Thus Germany might, by a skilful application of protective tariffs, conquer the markets of other countries and thereby gain the wealth wherewith to conquer the world.

The 20.000.000 Teutons, who at present inhabit the United States, Brazil and the Argentine, will have increased to, perhaps, a hundred millions, and, in the two Americas, their will may be Law.

CHAPTER X.

ENGLAND'S SECURITY A THING OF THE PAST. THE OLD DIPLOMACY.

These are a few political and economic aspects. But there are others.

As science advances, explosives will certainly be invented, whose power will exceed that of dynamite in the same, or in a far greater degree than dynamite exceeds gunpowder in destructive effect.

We have to bear in mind that England's naval supremacy, what with the perfection of aircraft and of submarines, will fairly soon be another romantic recollection of a bygone age. After all, England is a small country, and in a few more generations she will be outnumbered by many a land. Her fleet will be quite unable to do for her what it did in the heroic past, because aicraft and submarine will be infinitely more formidable than they are now. There may be any European coalition against England; and far from being invulnerable on her islands, the sea will enable her enemies to attack her from all sides, unseen, and relentlessly. Nothing can prevent Germany from building thousands of Super-Zeppelins and any number of amphibious aircraft.

In any case then, an old-fashioned peace will not leave the world much better off than it was before 1914, and in many respects even a good deal worse.

As before the war, the Moral Code of the State will differ with that held sacred by the individual; when the State commits an injustice, it will have to soothe the scruples of its millions by lies, by phrases, by hypocrisy.

Each state will be afraid of its neighbour or it will covet its possessions or its territory, or its trade. For many years, wars in Europe may be avoided; but fear and aggression will do their work like they did in the 20th century. And in the meantime international intercourse will not be what it should be.

For the old, old, fallacy, that the various nations and states have conflicting interests, like most superstitions, will be repeated and looked upon as an irrefutable truth; and each state will shape its policy accordingly. No Government will take the slightest notice of the general interest of Mankind; but each will only follow those dictates of a narrow and sordid provincialism, which are called, collectively, "national interests."

And again, fear will reign as supreme as aggression.

Strong States, threatened by stronger States or coalitions, will have to relinquish their role of protectors of weak ones, whom they will be obliged to leave to the mercy of other States who will trample on their bodies as well as on their very souls. International Law will, as now, chiefly become remarkable by being violated and by giving belligerents an excuse for mutual vituperation for so doing.

Is there any man, then, who could view the future resulting from an old-fashioned peace without dismay and grave apprehension? There may be some, and not a few, it must be feared, amongst professional politicians and government officials, who, from sheer force of habit and moral stolidity could not be bothered with novel notions about polities. They prefer to stay in the atmosphere of mistrust and of national egotism, in which they have always breathed. They honestly believe, perhaps, that the world is incorrigible. We do not intend to speak badly of them. They have done, and will surely do, that which they consider to be their duty as honest servants of their State. That is the highest tribute that can be paid to them, and the highest they hope for, or aspire to. But for all that, they have been utterly helpless to avoid the calamity of our time, and they have all contributed something towards bringing it about.

The ways of diplomats are strange. When Bismarck thought that the other man expected that he would tell him a lie, he told him the truth. The other man then acted upon the reverse of what Bismarck said and lost the game. Then Bismarck posed as a truthful man, and the other looked rather foolish. I have known an old gentleman who was minister somewhere but was called back to his capital to be "Directeur du bureau du Ministère des affaires étrangères." His chief duty was to say to visitors: "mon cher Monsieur, nous n'en savons rien du tout". — There is a saying in England that a diplomat is a man who is sent abroad to *lie* for his country. — A French diplomat, being asked what "non-intervention" meant, said it meant: "non intervention" but sometimes it meant "intervention". — An old-fashioned peace will keep all this mediaeval nonsense on its pedestal of "diplomacy." When will society sweep the old rubbish aside?

CHAPTER XI.

THE PASSING OF POLITICAL MORALITY AND ITS REDEMPTION.

It may be perfectly true that Germany's megalomania and ultra-militarism are the preponderating causes of the War. But who can deny that the annexation of the Boer Republics by Great Britain lowered the standard of international political morality, or that it blunted the subtle distinctive feeling of right und wrong in the world? And that it made an impression on the world of fifteen years ago which was similar to that which Belgium's destruction has made on the world of 1915, true, not similar in *intensity*, but similar in character? We are only too ready to admit that the comparison is anything but perfect; England had not guaranteed the Boer Republics, the Boers had more faults than even their friends in Holland cared to admit; South-Africa is better off now than before the war. But still, an *injustice* was done! There's the rub. Germany had to stand by. Her people had to be satisfied with giving vent to their feelings in print, being powerless to go any further. For as long as Germany possessed no naval power of sufficient strength to give her a voice in all international affairs, she could not make her material interests respected; and when a wrong was perpetrated in the world, she was no more able to oppose it than Switzerland. That was intolerable. Thus, from a variety of causes, of which certainly megalomania was not the least patent, Germany became Britain's rival on the sea. Was Britain always free from Germany's faults? Did not Britain desire what *she* called *her* "Cultur" to predominate? Did not Britain think light of the rights of others when she considered her own material interests at stake? Recent history is there to answer those questions, and fair-minded inquirers can but quote the Great Thinker's words: "Let him, who is without sin, throw the first stone".

The same applies to Russia, to France, to Japan, to every great power, even to the small powers. Whenever their interests were considered in danger, down came their mailed first, which is by no means an exclusively German patent.

We need not quote further examples, for past History abounds in Boer States and Belgiums and Polands. We may ascribe to our readers enough historical knowledge to enable them to count them by dozens in the history of the last two centuries. In fact, the civilised world has become so thoroughly used to them, that if Belgium had not happened to be a country representing an ancient civilisation, full of its wonderful monuments, and if these monuments had been carefully shielded from destruction and the populace treated in a manner approaching decency, the violation of Belgium's neutrality by itself would have roused the world's virtuous indignation and no more.

The statesmen of all countries, as we have just remarked, have all contributed at least something towards bringing the present calamity about. And yet, when it came at last, they have all, indignantly, repudiated all responsibility for it. This shows, for one thing, that they are ashamed *as men*, of their actions *as statesmen*, and that statesmen, from the very nature of international relations, are unable to avert disasters like the European war.

Those relations, of course, are based upon an assumption which is fundamentally wrong, and which holds, that the interests of the various nations and states are conflicting.

We are of opinion that this superstitious idea should be got rid of as soon as possible and we hold, on the contrary, that so far from having conflicting interests, the nations of the world have One Great Common Interest, which is: the conquest of Nature by the knowledge of its Eternal Laws. This Great Truth must be adopted as a lofty political creed; a practical religion, which descends to the worldly needs of the commonwealth of States; a faith which even *statesmen* may honestly believe in *and act upon*, without either being hypocrites or perverting their conscience; a religion which chooses International Parliament as its place of worship, and the Code of International Law as its Holy Book.

In order to give the reader a clear notion of our point of view and of what, in our opinion and according to our firm conviction, is the ultimate destiny of Man, we must now discuss what we prefer to call the religious aspect of human life, and in doing so, we shall, at the same time, elaborate some of the Aphorisms with which we have opened this essay.

CHAPTER XII.

THE EAST AND THE WEST.

From time immemorial the great thinkers of Mankind have proclaimed ideas which, though clothed in different words, and elucidated by different metaphor, proved a common origin. The great value, attached to those ideas, lay in the fact that they regulated the behaviour of men to each other. They all tended *to make the best of life.* They are, in all great religions, the same and we call them, collectively, Moral Law. There cannot be the slightest doubt, that as regards this Law, as regards its fundamental precepts, all world-religions teach the same principles, amongst which we find preservation of human life, mutual aid and love, honesty and truthfulness, respect for personal property, parental and filial love, and the holiness of matrimony universally accepted, and admitted as axioms which need no discussion.

These principles were all the more easily accepted, when they were proclaimed by persons, who, from their personal appearance or by their striking eloquence, or by their poetic gifts, and by the magnetic influence they knew to exercise over their audience, were known to be mysteriously connected with the Supreme Being. They were the great prophets, the founders of religions.

The human mind, as proved by untiring scientific research, covers two regions: conscious and unconscious thought. The former belongs to the individual: matter, come into temporary consciousness, during personal life. The latter belongs to the race, and together with it, to the Universe, to God, and knows not of time nor space. Conscious thought represents one man, unconscious thought represents Mankind, which is God, become conscious, of which each individual is an infinitisimal part, like a drop in an ocean. We find this thought beautifully expressed in a sublime Persian poem, translated by Prof. Browne:

".... Beware, say not: He is All-Beautiful,
And we His lovers'. Thou art but the glass,
And He the Face confronting it, which casts
Its image on the mirror. He alone
Is manifest, and thou in truth art hid.
Pure Love, like Beauty, coming but from Him,
Reveals itself in thee. If steadfastly
Thou canst regard, thou wilt at length perceive,
He is the mirror also, He alike
The Treasure and the casket. 'I' and ,Thou'
Have here no place and are but phantasies
Vain and unreal. Silence! for this tale
Is endless, and no eloquence hath power
To speak of Him. 't Is best for us to love.
And suffer silently, being as naught."

Jami, the greatest of all Sufi poets of Persia, that ancient land, where men have thought deep thoughts almost since the dawn of civilisation, in this wonderful poem gives us his confession of Faith, of his simple, deep and noble religion which the East has never forgotten, the East, that Treasure-House of Human Thought!

The Germans complain that the Asiatic troops are "dusky savages" let loose upon them by the Allies. Could any taunt be more monstrous and grotesque than this, coming from the people whose soldiers ravaged Belgium like a pack of wolves? Here we have the mental attitude of Europe at her worst *in all its imbecile arrogance!*

Wrestling with reluctant nature to conquer her, forgetting all the rest, forgetting even her noble self in the fray, the West lost her soul.... for a time. She will find it back as soon as she returns to the Holy Books that the East alone could give her. She has been away from home, on a journey of discovery.

The Ancients looked upon dreams as manifestations of divine thought. The interpretation of dreams was entrusted to men of the highest character. The Ancients knew that sleep opens the gates of the soul, a truth which only modern science of our day has revealed once more. And so they lent a ready ear to all those who uttered deep thoughts which came to them in a dreamy state of extasy. We know now that they were right in declaring that the words of the Prophets were the words of God. The Greeks knew this so well that they erected a separate Altar to the "unknown God". They knew that all religions were manifestations of the Universal Mind, of God.

Modern science has revealed another truth, well known in Antiquity. Dreams, those strange emanations of unconscious thought, often present themselves in symbolic forms. And only those who possess sufficient penetration, can decipher their meaning. Most poets and seers have expressed their thoughts in a symbolic manner. Perhaps this proves the fact that we can only understand things by their relation to other things, because they are all One. And it has truly been said, that we should look upon the world and upon life as upon one immense concert, of which we, small particles of the Universe, can only hear the few notes in our vicinity, but we fail to hear the Harmony of the whole. But unconscious thought knows neither time nor space, being universal and divine, and for it all things are One.

CHAPTER XIII.

THE WHITE MAN'S MARTYRDOM.

The unconscious thought of Mankind will ultimately guide it along the right path. In his unconscious Self Man has known that the Seers were right, that the Moral Laws which they proclaimed were, as far a the life and the destiny of Man are concerned, *absolute*.

Europe, when it acknowledged the sublime doctrines of Christ as Divine Truths, obeyed her unconscious Self. But she knew, that the time was not ripe for making realities of them. Yet she cherished them, in her heart, and upon them in olden days she lavished all her wonderful genius. Whilst the Church admitted that Man was a mixture of Mind and Matter, she allowed the flesh large concessions, as long as it would admit the superiority of the Spirit. Hence the marvellous beauty of the mediaeval churches, where the people paid fervent homage to their spiritual treasures by all the splendour of their artistic genius. The Church had made a magnificent poem of the teachings and the life of Christ and round them her Saints and Sages had entwined all manner of romantic lore, at which the simple hearts of all true believers were gladdened and marvelled greatly. The Church for them was the world, a great, roomy, strong house, in which they were safe in life and after death for evermore. Even Emperors whose material wealth and power knew no limit, were her servants. Those were the days of Canossa. Bismarck once declared they would never return. Matter would not be ruled by Mind, a new era had come, he and his country thought, in which the flesh would rule the spirit.

In the Middle Ages the History of Europe, the History of civilisation itself was the History of the Church, She represented all that was pure and noble in Europe. When the Portuguese and the Spaniards carried the White Man's civilisation over the oceans, the Church went with them and gave sanction to their work. The Church started the exploration of America and of Africa and Asia. When an Emperor or a King annexed a hitherto unknown land, he did so for the Church, for the Christian faith. And so the Church wove her golden thread through the fabric of civilisation and of society in the wonderful days of the Middle Ages. She had guided the steps of Europe, her child, her son. But he had eaten of the Tree of knowledge, which she, herself, had nurtured in her House. He had become acquainted with worlds beyond Europe, which she had bade him conquer for the Faith. And as he discovered the world beyond Europe and the lands unknown even to the Ancients, the world became less of a mystery to him. His mind had broadened, and as it was fed with fresh knowledge, it asked for more. It asked, in fact, for more than the Church cared to grant. The Church, guided by men, made countless errors. She wished, not only to withhold from Mankind such knowledge as she considered beyond its grasp, fearing that it would make an ill use of it. But she also forbade inquiry into the Mysteries of the Faith. When the Reformation had cleft Christendom asunder, the Church made more errors than before, until at last she returned to her own faith which holds that meekness will inherit the earth; it may be, that the Church of Rome will for ever forget the words: *non possumus*.

The White Man has been away, in search of unknown lands, in quest of hidden knowledge. He is master of the world; a thousand concealed treasures he has found. But his soul is bleeding from many wounds and yearns for home. The Son of the Church has returned, a grown-up man, of mighty frame; if she will only throw open wide her Gates, he will enter. If not, he will look for a new Home, or perish outside. And then the Church and Western civilisation will perish with him. The Tree of Knowledge which they have planted, will be worshipped by worthier and wiser races, who will know how to use its divine fruit, which only the Wise will taste in all its sweetness. The torch will change hands, but its light will still guide Man to a higher destiny. For he will never lose his faith in the future. He will not look for its foundation in the mystery of a phantastic past. He will find the strength of his splendid Hope in indisputable facts.

He knows that his Ancestors, long ages ago, were savages who have slowly risen to a higher level through the irresistable logic of the Moral Law which their soul evolved.

Knowing, that the improvement has been immense, he will also know that it will continue higher and higher to perfection.

CHAPTER XIV.

IF GERMANY IS NOT VANQUISHED.

We have, so far, discussed possible future developments exclusively from the point of view, and on the assumption, that the Allied Powers would be victorious, and that they would subdue Germany, after having penetrated into the country, and completely reduced its resistance. We have done so, because we assumed that it will hardly be possible to obtain Peace from Germany in any other way. This, of course, is merely an assumption, which should not make us lose sight of other possibilities.

At the beginning of the war, and until a few months ago, a victorious Germany was by no means unthinkable. But the splendid resistance made by France and Russia, the enthusiasm of all the British colonies and possessions, supporting the splendid bravery of the small Army which England, unprepared for war, could yet place at the disposal of her Allies and the certainty of conscription in England have reduced the chances of Germany and Austria to a minimum, which need not form a starting point for the discussion of the future at all; at least not in the sense that the aggressors could by any manner of means dictate the terms of Peace. Moreover, Germany's difficulties in obtaining supplies and breadstuffs will have a weakening effect upon that Power. Her financial position, as proved by the reduced value of the Reichsmark in neutral states, who continue exacting gold for the payment of goods, cannot be otherwise than extremely precarious. In view of all this, we may dismiss the assumption of a victorious Germany as unthinkable.

We should, however, consider other possibilities. In the first place it is quite impossible to predict, for how long Russia and France will be able, even with the greatest possible loyalty to the Entente, to keep up their tremendous effort. Poland and the North of France have been laid waste; they were amongst the richest regions of Russia and France. Belgium has been well-nigh ruined. And a further occupation of that unhappy land will make ruin more complete. As we have already remarked, Germany continues ravaging the territories she occupies with a complete insouciance as to who will pay the bill in the end.

It is, even if we admit that the resources of the British Empire are intact, an open question, whether even that Empire will be able to stand the strain of economic dislocation for an unlimited period of time. A hundred years ago, indeed, Britain could fight for twenty years without being ruined. But in our days a prolonged war will mean a very precarious situation for the world's commerce. On the one hand, there will be immense quantities of merchandise laid up, impossible to transport; on the other hand, some commodities will be so much in demand that their price will become prohibitive, sothat large industries will be doomed to inactivity. Take the case of Russian grain and American and Egyptian and Indian cotton. Supposing the next crops are gathered, before the existing ones are realised and consumed? We would probably see attempts at wholesale "*valorisations*" after the Brazilian style; but who could finance such operations, which, in time of peace, were difficult enough?

It is, for all these reasons, quite possible, that after another twelve months of war a general state of exhaustion and of moral depression will set in, which will pave the way for negotiations. This would jeopardize the future of Europe almost as much as a German victory, because an old-fashioned peace, with all its inherent potentialities for further strife, would then become unavoidable. German militarism would remain as truculent as ever, because it could not be accused of having been beaten.

At the time of writing, both groups are making frantic efforts for obtaining the help of neutrals, who are being influenced by alternate coaxing and bullying, by press-campaigns and diplomatic efforts in the good old style. With regard to the small neutrals, they have no reason to place any confidence in any assurances of future rewards, for they would have to deal with several powers, whose councils may be divided. They know, that International Law will be a farce after the war as much as it has been during it, and that their "interests" will only be considered if they happen to be identical with those of the mightiest combination of large Powers. They know, also, that if any of them, after a successful war, were to become at all powerful, the next war would be waged with the object of again reducing them, as their increased power would mean a threat to some neighbour somewhere. We need not give examples; history abounds in them. We do not mean to say that large States have always been wrong, or that they have been wrong at all. As long as there is no binding International Law, no International Law that can assert itself by united power, every State will act with supreme indifference to any ethical conceptions. There are, of course, a great many varieties of States, as in the past, all more or less dangerous to others and to their own subjects. There is, for instance, the State with the "historical mission"; the hard-working State that wants markets; the prolific State, which requires colonies; the State which is the Sole Proprietor of "Cultur"; the State, which yearns to make alle other States "free"; the dynastic State, which ruins itself in order to keep some imperial family in power; the State, which expects to be swallowed up by some powerful neighbour; the querulant State, constantly arming in fear of being "attacked"; the State which has an evil conscience; the insouciant State, which arms at the last moment, and appears an easy prey; the open-hearted State, which bluntly declares that it is there to fight and to destroy and to conquer; and so on, in an endless list of varieties, or of all or some combined. The State which has a "religious mission" is a more or less amiable recollection of the past.

If, therefore, the Entente Powers are perfectly honest in their assertions, that they desire to protect nationalities; that they wish to place the position of small states upon an unassailable foundation; that they wish to destroy the military power of Prussia, because that power is a constant threat to the peace of the civilised world; they cannot wish for a better moment for showing the honesty of their purpose than this. They can call a Congress together, with the avowed purpose of forming the Union of Europe and of creating the conditions under which International Law will reign supreme over all political ambitions, on the lines to be presently set forth. And in so doing, they will secure the co-operation of all neutral States. These would then have to throw their combined weight into the scale where the Union of Europe had been placed. And the further the attrition of Germania had gone, the greater the neutral influence for good would become.

CHAPTER XV.

INCORRIGIBLE GERMANY.

From the foregoing we may now draw our conclusions.

Whatever may be the terms of an old-fashioned peace, it will with absolute certainty contain the germs of further strife and of other wars, which will cause a great deal more devastation than the present one; the devastating and demoralising effect of these wars will grow in intensity with the growth of knowledge. And in the end the nations which together form Western Civilisation, will share the fate of all other nations or agglomerates of nations, which, in the past, were bellicose and aggressive: they will lose their wealth and their power, as they will destroy each other; and with them, Western Civilisation will disappear. The store of knowledge of this civilisation will pass on to other races, most probably to the Asiatics, who will make a better and more humane use of it. The White Man will have played his role as the discoverer of the world and of the foundations of human knowledge, and he will have perished in the attempt.

As to Great Britain, it may safely be predicted,

that with the coming perfection of the flying machine and the submarine, she will be no more secure against attack and destruction than any other power. She will remain inferior in numbers to the Teutons and she will not be able ever to oppose their attacks from the air with any permanent chance of success. An anti-British Continental coalition would make her position infinitely worse. Such a coalition is quite possible whenever some continental Power produces a Statesman of exceptional political genius, and his existence does not coincide with that of a man of the same calibre in England. As an example we may cite Louis XIV who did not succeed in subjugating Europe as he was effectively opposed by William III.

An old-fashioned peace will mean a continuation of the divergence of political and personal morals. Each individual state will take no heed of the material or other interests of other states.

No international agreement or promise will hold out against international hatreds or jealousies. As soon as a State believes itself or the coalition of which it is the head, powerful enough, it will not take the least notice of International Law, or of any human or „divine" laws whatever. It will break the peace and try to conquer by force what it cannot obtain otherwise. And this for the simple reason that its statesmen know that all the others, in their situation, would do precisely the same thing, and that if they did not take action at the right moment, the others would steal a march upon them and destroy them.

There is no doubt that all leading statesmen know that this is the real situation. But it would be absurd to say that they, all of them, like it to continue.

It is, however, very likely that the Emperors of Germany and Austria, and their advisers, who have made militarism their chief occupation in life, look upon war as a sport. The Monarchs themselves certainly never risk their own lives in battle. To them war is a very interesting scientific sport, in which they risk even less than if they played at football. To them, also, war is the study of a life-time, which takes up all their mental capacity. They have libraries full of books all about organised murder. They do not think in individuals, but in Army corps, and if they go rather much into detail, they think in batallions only. But in their science the individual is no more than a cog on a wheel. *It follows hat their mental attitude is perverted, that their mind becomes warped.* We may take it for granted that the Emperors of Germany and Austria, the Kings of Baden, Bavaria etc. will consider life hardly worth living without the sinister organisations of which they are the proud leaders. As long as separate States exist, whose "interests" are conflicting, they will have the strongest possible argument for the maintenance of arrangements for organised murder. They will continue to call military courage the only courage worth mentioning. They will say it, and have it said and printed so often, that their foolish subjects will believe them and continue to black their boots for them and think it an honour. Nobody will have the courage to tell them that military courage, as shown by troops in action, has no moral value whatever, save in exceptional cases, because this courage is generally engendered by blind excitement, fanaticism, rage, fear of officers or fear of being despised; and that this kind of courage cannot bear comparison with the quiet courage of peaceful men who bear undeserved blame without a murmur, who risk their lives in laboratories and hospitals or voyages of discovery, and often without the faintest hope of reward except in their own hearts. Nobody will dare to tell the monarchs that they ought to look for better occupation than organising murder, and that they had better lead Mankind towards peace than towards strife. They and their advisers and all their caste are incurable. They are steeped in egotism, vanity and in contempt of their subjects and of those who do not belong to their damnable faith and caste. They will go on hoodwinking their subjects with hollow phrases. Their subjects, poor fools, will lick the boots that kick them, and if they had tails, they would wag them.

Enough, dear reader, let us draw the curtain over this sorry piece of human perversity, vanity and stupidity. One day, it will belong to the past and it will sleep for ever in the limbo of vanished follies and crimes, together with cannibalism, torture and superstition.

It cannot be too often repeated, that Germany's attitude, with regard to Ultra-Militarism, so far, is incorrigible. The neutral press is constantly being flooded with demonstrations in favour of it. The Germans are now endeavouring to hide their abortive attempt to obtain the paramountcy in Europe, for which, indeed, Ultra-Militarism is a *sine qua non*, behind the argument, that a disarmed Europe would soon become a prey to conquerors from outside. They point to Japan, to the United States and to Russia, as representing the future dangers to European civilisation.

Whilst being fully convinced, that those dangers, if they exist at all, even in a latent state, are shrouded in the mysteries of the future, we would yet never represent a disarmed Europe as a „consummation devoutly to be wished". This much, however, is quite certain, that Europe will decline to accept Germany as her leader in defending her. For Germany, in precipitating this war and in carrying it on without regard to International agreements and the dictates of Moral Law, has for ever forfeited her right to leadership. That honour can never be conferred on the Power which has tried to dominate Europe by devastating Europe. The sooner the Germans recognize this, the better. For not until they do, will it be possible for Europe to recognize Germania once more as her partner or as her daughter in the great work of Civilisation. At present the Germans are still entangled in the strange delusions which they in their madness conceive as realities. They cannot conceive a courage which is not military courage; they cannot conceive a State which is not based on Ultra-Militarism; they cannot conceive Mankind working its way towards betterment and salvation in any other way than that of mutual slaughter, as the only means to secure the survival of the fittest; they cannot conceive that Mankind, being God or Nature come to consciousness, has the Power to alter its methods, and to replace them by others. They are incapable of looking upon Man otherwize than as a beast, with all its blind instincts, ruled by some outside power. They decline to recognise the fact, that all the world's work, these last fifty thousand years or more, centres in Man's great Endeavour to lift himself up to a higher level; *to substitute his own methods* for the cruel, blood-stained ways of blind Nature, and that the present resistance of Europe is but a link in the long chain of those attempts.

It would certainly be foolish to claim for the Entente Powers the monopoly of righteousness. Europe has not forgotten French domination in the time of Louis XIV and of Napoleon, and the devastations wrought upon her in their days. South Africa has perhaps forgiven, but not forgotten the Great Boer War. Persia knows something about Russia at her worst, perhaps more than is convenient at present.

Even our own Holland has not conquered Insulinde i. e. the Malay Archipelago by the gentle art of persuasion.

But none of the European Powers has ever been guilty of so revolting and so foul a treason as Prussia's sudden onslaught on Belgium, whose safety she had sworn to protect. It is not too much to say, then, that Germany, led by Prussia, represents European civilisation at its worst. And unless Europe succeeds in abolishing Prussianism, her civilisation will be lost.

CHAPTER XVI

NATIONS AND STATES

It is exceedingly difficult to define the meaning of the word *nation*, with regard to the sense in which it is generally used, because everything depends upon whether the sense is political or ethnographic.

We often hear of the Belgian nation, of the British nation, of the American nation, of the Jewish nation. And yet in each case the word really means a different thing.

The Belgian nation consists, roughly, of two entirely different peoples, the Flemish, whose native tongue is Dutch, and the Walloons, whose native tongue is a very ancient Romance dialect. The Flemish are a Teutonic race, the Walloons are of Gallic descent. They are, therefore, in race, in language and in character, entirely different. They have, however, the Roman Catholic faith in common. They were united into one State by the Congress of Paris in 1831. None of the two races can be said to have subjected the other in any way. Instead of the one having forced its language upon the other, they have adopted French largely as their common language. although

French and Dutch (Flemish) are the two official languages.

Whereas Walloon has almost disappeared as a literary language, Flemish has never ceased to exist and to develop in that sense.

In the United Kingdom we find, as far as England, Scotland and Wales are concerned, a common language and a common religion. Only Ireland, partly, belongs to the Roman Catholic faith, and its peasant population still speaks its ancient language. And yet, Scotch, Welsh, and English each look upon their own race as quite distinct from the others, as much as the Irish do.

In the United States of North America we find a common language, English, and a common religion, but the greatest possible diversity of race. Yet there is not a single American citizen who is not proud of being one. The war has indeed proved that many German-Americans still feel much for their old country; but the overwhelming majority are American citizens first and Germanophiles only in the second place.

Different from all these are the Jews. They are not in possession of any particular land, they have no common material interests. Owing to their having lived in different countries for centuries, they show, even ethnographically, very marked differences. But they have a common religion and a common language and origin, and they constitute indeed the Jewish nation. They have done so for thousands of years, and no vicissitude has shaken their feeling of belonging to a common nationality.

The conviction that all the Jews in the world form a nation is equally strongly felt by the Jews themselves as by outsiders and the fact is so positive that we may consider it as of very great importance.

From it we may safely conclude, that, primarily, "material" interests have very little to do with nationality. Religion, when not a universal religion, but retained by one particular race as its own, as is the case with Israelites, is a very strong tie, and so is language. These two bring individuals together more than anything else, and hence nationalities may consist of more than one race, as long as they have religion or language in common.

Now the conception of a State, as we have seen in the case of Belgium, Great Britain and the U. S. A., and as we may observe with equal conclusions in the cases of Russia, Austria-Hungary, Persia, China and many other countries, does not by any means coincide with that of a nation.

In Russia, Germany and Austria, for instance, separate nationalities like the Finns and the Poles look upon the State as their enemy and oppressor. If the Poles were possessed of certain qualities which together make politically creative force, they would, if the present war afforded them a chance, make their nation into a State, in the same way as the Bulgarians, Servians, Roumanians and other nations did who were previously oppressed by the Turks.

What is a State? It is almost as difficult to define the notion of a State as of a Nation.

In neither case can it be said that numbers form the chief attribute. The Russians number almost twenty times as much as the Belgians or the Roumanians. Londen is a town or city but it has more inhabitants than Holland and twice as many inhabitants as Denmark, and more than the whole of Scandinavia. Yet Holland has large colonial possessions, and Scandinavia like Holland, has developed its own art and literature. Again, Paris, holding not a twentieth part of the population of France, has always played the chief role in French History. Carthage, Venice, Genua, Amsterdam were cities with no more than a few hundred thousand inhabitants. Yet their embassadors were as proud as Spanish Grandees, and they would wage war with the mightiest lands.

It is curious, at the same time, that the farther we go back in history, the more we find small States or indeed mere cities, playing an international role which their size as compared to that of their neighbours seems to forbid. The fact is, of course, that, e. g. in the Middle Ages, and up to the Napoleonic wars, fighting was done chiefly by hirelings, who had made war their *métier*. Credit was much less developed than it is today, and he who had the most ready cash could obtain the most soldiers.

In those days the people at large abhorred war and figthing much more than they do now in Germany. They would never have thought of ascribing to war any noble or inspiring qualities, as has been done by many authors of our day, especially of course in Germany. They got a separate class of men to do the beastly and disgraceful work for them. They paid them well, but they felt nothing but contempt for them. Soldiers, in those days, were men who possessed no religious or humane feelings whatever, who robbed and murdered whenever they got the chance, and were believed by all honest people to be destined for the most thorough eternal perdition. Good women, when they passed, would make the sign of the cross.

But from the time of Napoleon onwards all this has changed. France has been the first country to make patriotism a religion, and Napoleon's immeasurable ambition could wish for no better companion than French patriotism. Conscription and standing armies alone could furnish him the power he was yearning for. Patriotic megalomania which has in our time manifested itself in German ultra-militarism, was first shown by France, *la grande nation* as she called herself. France held Europe under her iron heel, she used her mailed fist, a great deal more than Germany is ever likely to do!

If we find it difficult to give a definition of what a State is, the State has no hesitation whatever in asserting itself and letting us know, especially since conscriptions and standing armies have become time-honoured institutions.

The most conspicuous attribute of a State, then, would appear to be military power (by land or by sea), and roughly it may be said of European States that their power increases with their number. Hence the romance of cities or very small states waging war successfully against much larger ones single-handed, belongs to the past. The question of power has become a mathematical problem. A problem, too, of organisation and foresight. But modern military courage engendered by drill has nothing to appeal to the idealistic propensities of the mind. Neither has the battlefield or the havoc wrought by the machinery of modern instruments of slaughter and torture.

CHAPTER XVII

LARGE STATES

If the ultimate aim, then, of a State is military power and size, it may be asked whether either of these two have contributed to the happiness of its inhabitants and whether they, in themselves, constitute considerable elements, or elements at all for that happiness? If we inquire into the personal comfort and contentment of the inhabitants of large States we find them, speaking generally, below those of the people of small countries. There is much less poverty in Denmark or in Holland, on an average, than in Russia or in the United States. If this were not true, if the difference were in favour of the large states, there would be no small States at all, their inhabitants would all have either migrated to the large ones or have contrived a union. So far from wishing to do so, the small States have never asserted their desire for independance with more emphasis than in our day. The present war shows that the subjects of large States, like Russia and France, if they live anywhere away from the centre, are just as badly off as those of small ones like Belgium when war breaks out.

From the point of view of the individual, therefore, it may safely be asserted that the size of the State of which he is the subject, does not increase his personal comfort or contentment. In Germany the annual number of suicides is 17 per 100,000 souls. In Holland it is only 8 per 100.000.

From that same point of view, which can hardly be different from that of the whole of Mankind, it may be asked, then, whether large States are at all desirable?

We have seen that the Moral Code of a State, or rather the motives by which its servants are prompted, are in the most positive conflict with their individual morality. The State, in fact, has no conscience, and the individual Statesman, as such, has to behave as if he had none. It follows, that the greater the material force, the greater the military power, which is at the disposal of the State, the more gigantic will become the results of material force and of military power. And seeing that morals play no deterrent role, the wrongs and injustices which the large States will commit will tend to grow with the size of the State. The large State, as is evident in the case of Germany in the present war, assumes all the relentless, unreasoning, blind and deaf force of a hurricane or of an earthquake.

In regard to its power for wrong, therefore, the large State is a highly unsatisfactory institution.

In the case of Germany and Austria we have seen

that aggressive imperialism was caused by a highly composite state of mind, of which the chief component parts were Byzantinism, with its syllogistic resultants: ultra-militarism and megalomania, and that this state of mind was systematically nursed, at first by dynasties, and later on by entire schools of thought or philosophy, and that the inhabitants of the States in question ultimately looked upon themselves as possessed of the noblest virtues which patriotism could possibly engender.

In the case of other large states aggressive imperialism may not be caused, and has in most cases not been caused by the same fatal string of faults in the national disposition. But it has certainly been, and will be again and again, caused by those other monarchs, whom we often hear called the Kings of Trade and Industry. A combination of men of peculiar genius under favorable circumstances may, even in large and modern democracies such as the United States of North America of today and in the democratised Germany and Austria and Russia of tomorrow, bring about precisely the same state of mind as was inflicted upon the unlucky French people of Napoleon's glorious days, or upon the wretched millions of blind and misled Germania. In obtaining more territory and an increased population for their country the Kings of Industry will see fresh means of increasing their wealth and their power. By their newspapers and books and speeches they will incite their mobs as much as their hereditary namesakes in monarchical States have done before them. And the result will be more Belgiums ruined, more Polands devastated, more Boer States deprived of the immaterial treasure which they hold most sacred: independance, and of course more fruitless indignations, and more pecksniffian crocodile tears. But, as we have tried to point out, the devastations will be greater as science advances, the slaugther will be on a much more gigantic scale. Only the crocodile tears will flow at much the same rate. But the final result is bound to be the total collapse of European society.

Again, we must not deceive ourselves by optimistic dreams in regard to any supposed inherently peaceful disposition of democracies.

Whilst Mazzini held, that they mean progress under the best and wisest, Talleyrand, with withering contempt, called them aristocracies of roughs. Neither can it be denied, that, in the past, democracies, such as Athens, Rome, Carthage, have been bellicose and aggressive to a degree, and that in modern times France, in Robespierre's days, was more aggressive than even Louis XIV himself. In recent times, the war between Spain and the United States proved the democracy to be far from peaceful and meek, and the South-American republics seem almost to thrive on continuous quarrels.

Aggressive patriotism, therefore, is not limited to monarchic states only. King Demos may provoke war too. We believe, however, that the overwhelming majority of wars have been caused by dynasties and their interests. As in most wordly affairs, "*le genre humain n'est pas placé entre le bien et le mal, mais entre le mal et le pire*" and society will have to choose the lesser of two evils, if such they might be called.

Enough has been said, we believe, to show that out of a great many millions of individuals only a very few are favoured by the development of large states; that the great majority of men are happy or unhappy, absolutely irrespective of whether they belong to one large Empire or to another, and that their chance of contentment is even greater in a small state than in a large one; that whereas war will bring power and wealth to a very few only (to Emperors and Kings and a few high military and other officials in States like Germany and Austria; to the Kings of industry in democratic States) it means torture, death, misery and ruin to countless multitudes.

If it is not patent to the majority of thinking men from what we have seen in the present war, that this state of affairs is a disgrace to humanity, that it is pitifully ridiculous and absolutely intolerable, we may as well fold our hands and bide the doom of Western civilisation.

But there is no lack of strong sentiment on the subject, uttered in numerous books, pamphlets, and in the daily press of the entire world. Man is positively wrestling with a terrific evil, society is in travail and war is its labour-pains.

We know that in regard to their tremendous power for wrong, large States are highly unsatisfactory institutions.

But the large States are there. We cannot possibly get rid of them. We might as well try to get rid of mountains or oceans. They are in the nature of things. We might as well try to get rid of hurricanes or of earthquakes, as of wars, as long as the large States enjoy complete liberty. And as they are there before us, as gigantic facts, which cannot be talked or dreamed away, we shall have to make the best of them.

Although it is very difficult to give a satisfactory definition of the ideas: Nation and State, we shall have no difficulty in determining as one of the characteristics of a State the desire of power. This of course does not apply to all. It is more or less like a disease through which they have to pass. In the course of History many Nations or States have been known to keep peacefully within their boundaries for centuries and centuries on end. But suddenly they have an attack of insanity and they burst all bonds, which consist of friendly treaties, traditional relations, commercial ties etc. — We need only refer to Assyria, Media, Persia, Macedonia, Rome, Arabia, Turkey, and in modern times to Spain, France and Germany. All these countries have brought untold disaster on their neighbours and on themselves; in almost every case the object, in reality, has been the supposed or the real material advantage of the ruling dynasty and caste. No autocratic dynasty has ever ruled without attaching a great and influential caste to its interests. And this caste has "always contrived, either by force or by suggestive persuasion, to drive certain parts of the population to insane pugnacity". Neither have arguments been wanting to persuade the mob that they were doing wise and noble deeds in killing their neigbours and in robbing them as much as possible.

In some cases a favorite religion had to be spread. The Arabs used this as a pretext for looting to their heart's content, when Mohamed led them against the Unbelievers. They had Koran-texts which sanctified or appeared to sanctify all sorts of warlike actions. The Turks had no pretext at all, except, sometimes, the spread of Islam. But this only served to give free play to their predilection for the pastime of throat-cutting and for being, in a general way, objectionable. The Spaniards were great fighters; they had been fighting the Arabs for ages to get them out of their country and they had ended in becoming religious fanatics. This, the poverty of their land and a surplus of splendid energy led them to colonising enormous countries in South-America. But it also prompted them to terrible acts of atrocity in the Netherlands, which may only be excused by the sincerity of their religious fanaticism; they did not, however, devastate the Netherlands to anything like the same extent as the Germans have now devastated the Southern Netherlands, now called Belgium.

In other cases the real object of war has been cleverly hidden from view by holding up to the mob some phrase about the nation's duty to Europe, as in the case of France after the revolution, when France posed as the liberator of mankind. The French, the most highly gifted of all European races, had a tremendous surplus of intellect. They devastated a very great many countries and murdered hundreds of thousands of innocent people of their own and of other nationalities, but intellectually they enriched Europe. That is why the French have never been hated as a nation. Yet their megalomania, even down to 1870, was quite as bad, although not so unfounded, as that of Germany today.

England, on the whole, has been free of megalomania or of sudden attacks of insanity. She has obtained possession of the greatest empire the world has ever seen, in a very gradual way, and in an almost off-hand or absent-minded manner sometimes. The Boer War came as an unpleasant surprise to England's friends in the world, and however unavoidable it may have been, it lowered the moral standard of the mob. But a very large section of Public Opinion opposed the war and this as well as the generous treatment of South-Africa afterwards saved England in the eyes of the world.

But irrespective of motives or of ends, whether not

clearly defined, or well understood, small or large States, as soon as a certain necessary combination of circumstances was created, have behaved like natural phenomena, with an equally profound contempt for Moral Law, with an equally complete ignorance of Good and Bad.

Clearly, we cannot tolerate a state of affairs which allows large agglomerates of individuals to behave in this brutal and headlong fashion. We do not, from their earliest childhood, instil into the minds of our children principles of morals, of self-restraint, of altruism, of Christian virtue in short, that they may throw them to the winds and laugh them to scorn as soon as they know themselves supported by the majority of their countrymen. We cannot tolerate a state of affairs which makes each large State a potential enemy of the others and which engenders a constant feeling of mistrust and fear.

We shall have to convince nations and States that they can obtain the power they are yearning to possess, by peaceful means, in a perfectly honest way, at an infinite saving of treasure, misery and hatred.

After all, they are yearning for power in order to obtain more wealth and comfort, in order to extend the use of their particular language, the influence of their artistic and scientific schools, the sale of their wine, their shirtings, their toys, their electric plant, their autocars, in order to extend the scope for the realisation of their national energies and characteristics, sothat they may feel themselves at home in as large a part of the world as may be. At least this is what the mob, which has in the end to do the fighting and the dirty work, is told by the leading caste.

Especially in the case of conquering markets for the sale of manufactured goods the mob is easily moved, and not without some reason. European mobs are also moved by "national ideals" but these are more easily exported than manufactured goods.

CHAPTER XVIII

PROTECTION AND FREETRADE

Manufactured goods are kept out of countries by protective tariffs. — Tariffs do not always show the same effect everywhere. As a rule, however, in very large countries, like Russia and the United States, and to a great extent Germany, they have developed industry, that is to say they have enriched the proprietors of industries; on the whole, the mob, that is the labourers, are not very much better off than they were; not to anything like the same extent as the capitalists, but still to some extent, in accordance with the benefits they derive from labour organisation, social laws etc., in accordance, in fact, with the degree to which they have contrived to induce their employers to share profits with them.

It is quite superfluous here to discuss the merits of Free Trade and of Protection for any particular country. We have to deal with facts. The fact is that almost all Governments have adopted Protective Tariffs. They think that they are better off with them. But we have to put on record, that Free Trade if adopted universally, is now generally admitted to be by far the best Peacemaker, because it wil remove one of the greatest causes of international jealousy and friction.

So much has been written on this question that I may suppose the reader to be acquainted with its position, which is that universal adoption of Freetrade is admitted to be desirable and that this has assumed the weight of an axiom which needs no proof. — But as a lucid illustration of the interdependance of the nations and their industries and trade I cannot do better than quote Mr. Norman Angell in his address to the International Congress for Free-Trade, which was to be held in Amsterdam in September 1914, and in which he says: "What do we mean with "German" trade in an international sense? Take "the owner of an Ironworks in Essen, who builds "locomotives for a railway in an Argentine province "(for which railway the capital was found in Paris), "which railway has become necessary for exporting "wool to Bradford, where work has increased owing "to sales in the United States, which were caused by "the high prices obtainable there, owing to the deve-"lopment of agriculture in the West, which had ne-"cessitated the fertilisation of desert land now no "longer available for sheep-farming. If the money had "not been found in Paris, (which now is due to good "wine -and olive crops, which are chiefly sold in Lon-"don and New-York) and if the Bradford manufact-"urer had not required the wool, (he may have found "a market for woollen blankets amongst the miners in

"Montana who worked copper for a cable for China, "which cable had become necessary because the en-"couragement by the Republican Government in "China had caused Chinese Newspapers to print tele-"grams from Europe) if all these factors and an entire "chain of similar ones had not been at work, the "owner of the Iron Works in Essen, would have been "unable to sell locomotives."

Nothing could better convince the reader of the fact that the prosperity of one nation is of the greatest importance to the others in our time. It has not always been so. There were times when certain countries could monopolize a particular branch of trade and so enrich themselves. Holland, some centuries ago, could still monopolize the Spice-trade. But today trade is mostly carried on by companies whose shares may be purchased by anybody, on any stock -exchange.

Still, although already now, and even after an old-fashioned peace, the various States of the world will be as interdependent as ever, the fact that tariffs will be raised as so many walls to keep out alien trade, will remain, and will remain one of the chief causes of organised murder.

In the olden days, when money was unknown, trade was nothing but barter. One tribe possessed salt, another had fruit. So they made an exchange, and as a rule the one was no better off after the bargain than the other. But when money was invented, the character of the interchange of commodities changed from barter to trade. In the days of barter cunning was not necessary. A man could see precisely what he gave and what he got .But the invention of money complicated matters. You could only compare the value of commodities via money. As the value of money was much more stable than the value of commodities, money was wanted above all. It became necessary to have as much money and as few commodities as possible. When silver and gold were used as money-standards these developments accentuated themselves. Money became international. Although silver and gold are, in reality, commodities, they are the only commodities which even ultra-protectionist States admit free of duty. — It is the aim of every State to obtain money, above all other things. It follows that every State wishes to sell as much goods as possible and to buy as little as possible. Now, although individual traders wish the same, they behave differently. For they, also, wish to sell as much goods as possible, as they want money. Only, they do not care whether they get the money from their compatriots or from aliens beyond the frontier .It is a matter of complete indifference to them. Individual buyers, who buy goods only for personal use, are equally indifferent. They do not care whether the goods they buy, are made in their own land, whether they give their money to their compatriots or to aliens beyond the frontier as long as they think they get good value for their money. Evidently the interests of individuals are not those of agglomerates of individuals, called States. Therefore the State uses force. It compels its subjects to buy home-made goods, in making imported goods higher in price by levying duties. The interests of individuals, therefore, are *international*, the interests of the State are exclusively national. If, however, the State were to compel its citizens to divide their property equally amongst themselves, and to share profits equally, individual and State interets would be identical. But as equal division of money and property is impracticable, the two interests remain in opposition. This is one reason why the German idea of making everybody and everything subservient to the State, is a fallacy.

States which levy protective duties often succeed in fostering their home industries. This is proved by the prosperity of ultra-protectionist countries like Germany and the United States.

As the economical interests of States are exclusively national, whereas those of individuals are international, States behave in an ultra-patriotic manner. In order to obtain more duty, they want more markets, which they intend to surround by tariff-walls. They can only obtain such markets by conquest. They can make conquests only by military power, and in behaving themselves exactly like natural phenomena, with their complete disregard of all morality, as we have endeavoured to explain in the previous chapters.

Although the economic factor is not the only one responsible for international conflict, and although national vanity, ambition and Byzantinism, as we have seen, cannot be ignored, there is no doubt that it acts as a support to the others and as a bait, held out by the ruling caste to the ignorant mob.

If a system of international Freetrade could be thought out, we would at least have succeeded in freeing national aspirations from their materialistic, most egoistic and most ignoble propensities, and it is these which are so strongly felt by those who proclaim Freetrade as the great Peacemaker.

Now, when States can dispense with their enormous expenditure on armaments, they will have gigantic amounts at their disposal. These can be used, when Freetrade prevails, towards indemnifying those manufacturers whose business would suffer or become impossible, having been carried on hitherto solely or chiefly owing to the benefit conferred on them by protective tariffs. We need not here expatiate on all the merits of Free-Trade as against protection, from a theoretical point of view. Let us rather take a concrete case.

In 1902 (according to Mr. Geoffry Drage in his work "*Russian Affairs*", Londen 1904) Russia's imports and exports were as follows:

	Foodstuffs	Raw and half manufactured Goods	Animals	Manufactured articles	Total
Imports	£ 8,649,706	£ 31,395,069	£ 149,068	£ 15,810,000	£ 56,003,843
Exports	„ 55,906,519	„ 27,439,807	„ 2,292,662	„ 2,046,693	„ 87,685,618

Although Russia has adopted ultra-protectionism (the average *ad valorem* duty for British goods imported into Russia, e. g. is about 130%) she only exports for £ 2.046.693 of manufactured articles, but she is still obliged to import them to the value of about £15.810.000.—Although the excessive duty has enormously stimulated industry, and Russia now employs over 11.000.000 industrial male and female labourers, whilst over 93,000.000 persons of both sexes are employed in rural economy. *) all these people have to pay about twice as much, (and even more) for articles of clothing and other daily necessities (except corn and dairy produce) than their colleagues in freetrade countries like England and Holland. And, far from being better off than e. g. the labourers of the latter State, which is one of the smallest and least influential in the world, they are a great deal poorer and infinitely more miserable. It is a well known fact, that in Russia, which is the granary of Europe, and which exports for over £ 50.000.000 worth of foodstuffs annually, there are many districts where famine and diseases resulting from it, are permanent. We need but consult any author who is conversant with Russia's economical and financial position to know that in this unfortunate Empire the agriculturists are forced to sell their grain in order to pay their very high taxes, the State still keeping to the

*) G. Alexinsky-*Modern Russia* 1914.

famous principle which a Russian Statesman, in the bitterness of his heart, put into these words: "Nous ne mangerons pas, mais nous exporterons!" (We shall not eat, but we shall export).

Here then, we have the best type of an immense State, a State after the heart of the most passionate imperialist, covering a greater area than any other, having a larger budget than any other, more soldiers, more guns, more horses, more labourers, a bigger population, than any other.

But when we ask: what is the result, what is there to show for all these large-sized propositions, we cannot help arriving at the conclusion that in so far as the happiness, the contentment, of the overwhelming majority of the population are concerned, (*and, after all is said and done, these are the only things that really matter!*), Russia, the largest State in Europe, is one where more poverty, misery and desperation are found than in many others. The entire literature of modern Russia is there to prove it; there is scarcely a popular author in Russia today, whose novels do not show us types taken from the mob, heroes or heroines literally steeped in material and moral misery, who know not why they live, or what they want to do, or not to do, men and women without a wish or a will. The strikes, the increasing numbers of Nihilists, Anarchists and other malcontents prove it.

In this immense country we find, at every step

almost, our contention proved, that the interests of the individual are in direct conflict with those of the State as long as the State is managed by men who think they must conquer more territory and thereby more markets to monopolise. During the last 200 years Russia's history is made up almost exclusively of imperialism. Enormous territories in Asia have been added to the Empire, and all these territories have been jealously guarded, particularly since the latter half of the 19th century, against foreign trade. The tariff-wall has been built up higher and higher from year to year.

The financial and economic position of Russia is so terribly complicated, that even those, who have made a special study of it, find it exceedingly difficult to arrive at any definite conclusion as to the future. For our purpose, therefore, it cannot be useful to deal with it. But as to the *present*, there cannot be any doubt, that as far as the majority of the population is concerned, neither imperialism, nor protective tariffs have been conducive to its betterment, on the contrary, the majority is a good deal worse off than the majority in small States.

In Germany the situation is also very complicated. Here, also, however, the interests of the individual are in opposition to those of the State. We need but refer to the well-known conflict between the Agrarians, from whom the military caste which forms the ruling class in Germany, directly reponsible for the war, is recruited, and the socialists. The former produce food, which they wish to sell for high prices by aid of tariffs; the latter produce manufactured articles and have to buy dear food.

But Freetrade still reigned supreme in most of the markets of the British Empire, hence enormous quantities of German goods could be sold in those markets, which included England and all its colonies and possessions (with the exception, in some unimportant respects, of Australia and South Africa) with a population of about 400 millions of souls. But in England an influential minority clamoured for protection and it was quite possible although not probable that, in the long run, the protectionists would prevail. That would have been a calamity for Germany. Hence, economically, she felt herself at England's mercy. The liberal party in England, unconsciously perhaps, felt the difficulty and rather than rouse Germany upheld the principles of Cobden and Bright and strove to arrive at an understanding, which was on the very point of being concluded when the war broke out, which it could have done a great deal to prevent. For it would have disarmed the war-party in Germany to the extent of bereaving it of one of its arguments: Germany's economic dependence on the British Empire. We know now, of course, that even this would not have been sufficient. We know, that as long as Byzantinism and ultra-militarism prevail in Germany, all the understandings, economic or other, will not avert war. Even if Geat Britain had promised perpetual Freetrade, the German war party would not have been silenced.

If, therefore, we have introduced the economic factor in our general argument, we have only done so, in order to show that it plays a certain role, although by no means a decisive one, when we have to deal with States which are ruled by autocratic dynasties. For as we have pointed out, and as we see before our eyes, such dynasties may, in their exaggerated and vain ambition, carry large States and nations with them. They welcome the economic argument as a valuable addition to their arguments in favour of imperialism and ultra-militarism.

But, even if in the future, all autocracies were democratised, the economic argument in favour of conquest and war, will become more powerful than it is now, and in the hands of financial cliques and powerful Kings of industry, as we have already stated, will lead to international armed conflicts, whose magnitude and devastating effect will increase with the progress of science.

CHAPTER XIX

THE RESULTS OF AN OLD-FASHIONED PEACE

We may now state at what final conclusions we are bound to arrive, when we consider the results of an old-fashioned peace. They are:

1°. Treaties will be of value only as long as their terms suit the contracting parties. As soon as this is not the case, the party who thinks itself alone or in combination with others, powerful enough will repudiate them. This is true of all possible international treaties of whatever kind. Arbitration treaties are worse than useless, and even absolutely harmful, inasmuch as they tend to weaken the position of those States whose rulers put any trust in them, and thereby have a *bona fide* motive for lessening their preparedness for war. Such treaties, in fact, offer a premium for political immorality and hypocrisy.

2°. Autocratic Government engenders war.

3°. Protective tariffs ,combined with autocratic rule, make war absolutely unavoidable.

4°. Democratic Government without international Freetrade will not make war unavoidable or impossible.

5°. The protection of small nations will be a phrase without the remotest value.

6°. International crimes will be committed and no independent State will be obliged to interfere as long as its position allows it to shirk its moral responsibilities.

7°. International agreements concerning War, are useless because they would regulate actions which occur during a time of lawlessness and repudiation of all agreements.

There is a very great danger that an old-fashioned peace *will* be concluded. Foreign policy, even at this moment, is still carried on by each separate State, under the absolute control of "secret societies of diplomats." Many men of consequence have strongly objected to the abolition of secret diplomacy. Lord Cromer, in *The Times* of the 19th April 1915, declares — "In the great majority of cases the conduct of the "individual diplomatist merely reflects as a mirror "the public opinion and standard of national morality "of the people whom he represents, and there cannot "be any greater mistake than to confound Continen- "tal, especially German, and British diplomacy in one "general anathema."

We cannot help thinking, that for a diplomatist who represents a parliamentary State, it must be a matter of great difficulty to know public opinion in his country. In States like Great Britain, France, the United States, and in other countries governed by a parliamentary majority, public opinion is generally reflected in the press, of which about one half sides with the Government, whilst the other half is constantly engaged in abusing the party in power, and in describing its foreign policy, in unmistakable language, as a perfect abyss of folly and recklessness. We need but refer to the outcry in the British opposition press against the late Mr. Chamberlain's South African policy. — It has, unfortunately, to be admitted, that if the present war leads to an old-fashioned peace, there will be more need for secret diplomacy than ever; which will mean more phrases, more intrigues, more spies, more mutual deceit than ever. For can it be denied, that, in dealing with German diplomacy, to which, in Lord Cromer's opinion, the "general anathema" would be more particularly applicable, other countries will have to fight German diplomatic methods with their own objectionable weapons, and that, in so doing, they adopt the only way open to them, a way which their agents, as honest men, thoroughly detest and abhor? Can it be denied, that a diplomatist who acted in any other way, in order not to lower himself in his own eyes, would be a useless dreamer, if not worse? The fact is, that the abolishment of secret Diplomacy would be a dangerous thing for any country which carried it honestly into effect and that it can only be reached by States forming the Union of Europe, which we submit to be the only solution of the present crisis, and with which we propose to deal in the following chapter.

The mob does not care, as long as it has bread, clothing and a roof, and as long as it will be appeased by all sorts of phrases.

Large States will only protect small ones when it suits their interests.

When Philip of Spain tried to crush Holland, it suited England to crush Spain, by destroying the Armada in 1588. But Holland became a mighty State; and England, in the 17th century, fought her former protégé, who, in the 18th century, perished, an easy victim of French megalomania. I do not say that England is not now fighting for Belgium, and that, in England, there is not a very strong feeling of indignation; there can, indeed, be no doubt that but for this deep and fervent feeling of pity and anger, the British Government would find it ten times more difficult to carry on the war than they do now. For all that, England's honour, in this war, runs parallel with her interests, which forbid the establishment of a great Power in the Netherlands. As in the past, large States will protect small ones when they can do so without jeopardising their own interests; and when their interests are furthered by it, they are bound to do so. Beyond that, the small State will have to look out for itself and *remain armed to the teeth, or be victimised.*

CHAPTER XX

THE UNITED STATES OF EUROPE

If the present war has brought home any truth to the majority of thinking men and women, it is certainly this, that the state of Europe and of the world in general, is one of international anarchy, which no treaties or Hague conferences have been sufficient to palliate; and that its continuation, after the war, if an old-fashioned Peace shall have been concluded, will be certain, and disastrous to Europe in particular and to Western civilisation in general, which it will, eventually, destroy. If this destruction is felt to be undesirable for the welfare of Mankind, ways and means will have to be found to prevent it. They can only be found if all the States of Europe, and possibly the British self-governing colonies outside of Europe, and the United States of North America combine in unifying their interests.

In order to arrive at this result, we shall have to start with the Union of Europe, for this Union by itself would be so powerful, that all the other States would find it their interest to join them of their own accord.

It will be quite hopeless to expect the Union of Europe, unless, somehow, Germany and Austria are forced to disarm. We cannot for reasons explained in previous chapters, take any other point of view. But if the Entente powers were to propose the Union of Europe and an international army as a solution of the present crisis, it would be the duty of all the neutral powers to join them.

When making ourselves familiar with the conception of the United States of Europe, we should at once dismiss the idea that this Union could possibly be similar to the United States of North America, for although to all intents and purposes, European civilisation is one and undividable, sothat it is very difficult to „assess the contribution of each nation to the total fund of Western knowledge", the national idiosyncrasies of each race or State are so strongly marked, that it would be quite *impossible* for them all to be merged into one State.

Neither would it be *desirable* to bring this about, for diversity, and not uniformity is in the nature of things, and, especially in regard to nationalities, this diversity will assert itself against all obstacles.

Moreover, just as much as a certain amount of personal pride and self-assertion are indispensible for the well-being of the individual, patriotism if kept within certain limits, is highly desirable for every separate nationality. Patriotism tends to produce, by joint effort, by personal devotion, by pride of race, by a yearning for praise from compatriots, the highest endeavour towards the betterment of Mankind; for nations, in thus improving themselves, cannot but stimulate others to follow them. The preservation, therefore, of separate nationalities in Europe, must be considered as a question of extreme importance. Moreover, only a few nationalities lend themselves to centralisation of governmental power, because this tends to place supreme authority in the hands of certain cliques or castes; the larger the territory and population of such nations grow, the more will the divergence of individual and State interests be accentuated. In Russia, with her almost inconceivable diversity of races, languages and climates, the centralisation of administrative power has led to a chaotic state of the financial position, which tends to increase by the character of Russian officialdom. We make this remark without any feelings of partiality; but we have the Russians' own word for it in numerous publications asserting a highly unsatisfactory state of affairs. In such countries, therefore, local self-government is much to be desired; and if the Russian Government could be prevailed upon to allow nations like Poles and Finns, and possibly Georgia and Bokhara, to manage their own affairs under separate kings or local chiefs, who owe allegiance to Petrograd, it would be a step in the right direction, and worthy of a great and noble people.

Especially Poland deserves particular consideration. The Poles, who have been the pitiable victims of the rapacity of their more powerful neighbours for centuries, should once more be liberated and be allowed to develop all the splendid qualities of their national genius, which has never ceased to assert itself. The help which, in 1683, the Poles, headed by Sobieski rendered to Austria, when the Habsburg Emperor, instead of doing his duty, fled from Vienna, in mortal fear of the Turks, by itself is sufficient to prove Poland's eternal claim to Europe's gratitude. But for the Poles, Vienna and Austria would have fallen victims to Turkish barbarism, and history would have taken an entirely different course. But instead of earning gratitude, the talented and gifted Poles have been decried as a worthless and politically incapable nation, not worthy of a better fate than being an oppressed and subject race. During the present war this unfortunate people, divided over Austria, Germany and Russia, are forced to the heart-breaking task of fighting their own brothers, who speak their own language and have the same religion. If Western civilisation ever had reason to hide her face for very shame and disgust at an inhuman spectacle, it is here; of all the infernal atrocities of "Real-Politik" which the war has exposed in all its revolting ugliness, Poland, no less than Belgium, is the innocent victim. And not until Mankind, instead of invoking a powerless, because unthinkable Heaven, will recognise its own Soul as the supreme and all-powerful

Arbitre of human affairs, can we hope to see this crying injustice put right. If the great War were to bring that day nearer, it would indeed again be proved, that Evil sometimes is the raw material of Good.

Without in the least wishing to deprecate Russia, a country which bravely bears its share in the terrible task of liberating Europe from the Prussian nightmare, and whose soldiers show all the old courage and loyalty which have at all times been their conspicuous virtue, I would yet venture to submit that, first and foremost, the setting up of an independant Poland will be the *sine qua non* to the well-being of Eastern Europe.

As to Germany, as soon as the sorely tried subjects of the house of Hohenzollern will come to the conclusion that they have been disgracefully deceived by the cruel and shortsighted caste whose rule they have allowed to guide their destinies, we may expect a very great change in the mental attitude of that nation. They will have to understand that German Unity will never bring them the world-empire to which they aspire, but that, on the contrary, it would unavoidably cause renewed conflict in the future; that brute force, by itself, degrades and perverts the nations who make it their idol, and that the weapon which they have turned into a fetish, has struck down those who forged it. They will yet have to learn, that when their historians point to the old Germanic Empire of the Middle Ages as a political ideal which must be restored, these learned men have overlooked the immense strength of the Church in those days, and the significant fact, that the Emperor had to divide imperial power with the Pope. Thus, the Empire could not, and did not exist, or exert any power, when it was not held together by that subtle and invisible spiritual force which only a fervent faith in a universal religious belief could maintain; and in endeavouring to replace that faith by another religion: patriotism, supported by the blind force of ultra-militarism, Prussia has set itself an impossible and nefarious task, bound to lead to disaster, and to the perversion of German mentality.

Many Germans, no doubt, would feel greatly offended, if they were told that as a race, the Teutons lack political ability. And yet, when we read their history, we cannot help arriving at that conclusion. After the disruption of the Empire of Charlemagne there has never been any real German political unity as in France or England. The Emperors could not rule without the help of Rome. They needed it against the ambitions of the princely houses who elected them; and the latter welcomed the Reformation, and saved Luther's life, not from any religious sentiment, but chiefly because they knew that they would strengthen their own position in weakening the Spiritual power of Rome. It was the political immaturity of the Germans as a nation, which made them easy victims of the local dynasties before whom they loved to bow their submissive heads.

It was their fault and their misfortune, that the Reformation plunged their country in endless wars and thereby put Germany back two centuries behind her western neighbours. The German *psyche* which in a previous chapter we have endeavoured to define as badly balanced between the extremes of command and obedience, is still the same as it ever has been, otherwise they would not accept the farces of a powerless *Reichstag* and of a feudal *Landtag*, as if these were equivalents of representative institutions in other constitutional countries. Even in our time, Union could only be brought about by brute force, and it was Prussia which forced Bavaria, Saxony, Hanover and all the rest of them to recognize the Hohenzollerns as Emperors, much against their own wish. And if the present war results in an fearful national disaster, the Germans themselves, and their naïve addiction to being hoodwinked by *phrases* will have to bear the blame. Europe has not been partly ruined and devastated, not to feel convinced that it cannot again place huge powers into the hands of a race which only knows how to abuse them.

Hence, if even after the great national disaster which appears unavoidable, the Germans do not of their own accord return to decentralisation, for instance, by offering the imperial crown to some popular Prince as the hereditary but strictly constitutional head of a federation of constitutional kingdoms, they will have to be forced to it. Each German kingdom will have to become a separate entity, owing no allegiance to any of the others, and the kings of Prussia will have to relinquish the imperial crown, which will have to be a thing of a romantic but regrettable past.

The Germans, in the United States of Europe, will have the same opportunity for asserting their national existence as any other race. There is no reason whatever, to think that they will produce fewer thinkers, fewer men of learning, fewer artists, than before Prussian domination perverted their innate characteristics.

It may be argued, that a divided and politically powerless Germany would make too weak a screen against Moscovite ambitions, or against the ambitions of any other state, which today may appear harmless, but which may at any future time suddenly be caught by that craze of conquest which we know to be an endemic disease of live nations.

But in the United States of Europe, a Union of independant States, treating all their foreign affairs in an International Parliament, and policed by an International Army, such outbreaks would be impossible, if the Union of Europe could be brought about on the lines to be presently explained.

Apart from this, however, we should not lose sight of the fact, that Russia is gradually developing into a constitutional State, and that the decentralisation recommended above, is pleaded by many influential and prominent Russians whose voice may carry much more weight after the war than before it.

It must be well understood that the Union of Europe cannot be achieved, unless the principle of Freetrade is admitted as a *sine qua non*, not only as regards European States, but also with regard to their colonial possessions.

Although we should not advocate any curtailment of the individual sovereignty of each State, there ought certainly to be a maximum of uniformity in respect to the form of government. We have to place ourselves on the point of view, that even although democracies may not be quite free of aggressiveness, they will certainly prove to be that form of government which, coupled with interstate Freetrade, offers the least possible chance of international conflict. The States forming the Union of Europe will, therefore, have to be republics with chosen or hereditary heads; the former with a constitution like that of France, the latter with one like that of Holland or Belgium.

Their constitutions may vary a great deal in accordance with national characteristics and traditions; but they should all have some articles in common, of which the principal ones are:

1. All interstate relations are carried on in an International Parliament in which each State is represented by 5 members, who reside permanently in the place where that Parliament has its Site, e.g. at the Hague, which has already become the traditional centre of the study of International Law.

2. The 5 members representing each State must be appointed by the chosen representatives of the people from their midst. They receive fixed salaries which are uniform for them all. The salaries must be such that persons who are not possessed of private means are not excluded, but can live in a way consistent with their dignity.

3. The State shall not conclude any treaty with an extra-European State without submitting it to the International Parliament for its approval and publication. Secret treaties or clauses are void. All existing treaaies must be submitted to the International Parliament and will be void unless rafitied by it.

4. The State maintains no armed force by land or by sea or river of a greater strength than that which is required for the maintenance of order within its territory. The total may not exceed one per thousand of the population.

5. In its possessions or colonies outside Europe the State shall maintain no armed force beyond that which it employs at present. If the State desires to extend that force, the approval of International Parliament will be required.

6. The State shall manufacture no arms or war-material of any kind, nor allow the manufacture or import of them, either within its territory or within its colonies or possessions outside Europe, except by the express permission and under the strict control of the International Executive Council.

In England, where no written constitution exists, these articles may take the shape of special Acts of Parliament.

The conclusion of the Peace which is bound to be the outcome of the present war, will afford the best possible occasion for the constructive work of creating the constitution of the United States of Europe.

It would be a tremendous calamity if the impression were to gain ground, that this could wait until later. "Later" would be too late, and would mean more wars, more destruction and the downfall of Western civilisation. I must admit that when the downfall came, it would be fully deserved and that it would be quite the best thing that could happen to the rest of Mankind.

Evidently, if Peace is to bring us the United States of Europe, it will be necessary to convene not only the belligerents (1) but also all the neutral States of Europe and the United States of North America, to a Congress where the damage done by Germany and Austria in Belgium, the North of France, Poland and Servia may be assessed and the two Germanic Powers, their guilt of having been the aggressors being established, will be condemned to pay an immense sum to the victors, possibly several millards Sterling. Some readers will consider this phantastic, but when it is remembered that France had to pay 200 millions Sterling nearly half a century ago, and that the fighting armies are much more than ten times as large as in

(1) Including the British self-governing colonies.

1870, a figure of 3 or 4000 millions Sterling is not so extravagant, for the damage done to property by the Germans and Austrians far exceeds anything known in History. Even the destruction wrought by the hordes of Jinghiz Khan in the 13th Century in Asia and in Russia and Hungary cannot have been on anything like the present scale, except, perhaps, in Khorassan and some other parts of Central Asia which have never recovered; we are reminded of the sad fate of those countries by the statement recently published, regarding some parts of northern France, said to be so completely ruined as to be uninhabitable, and likely to be avoided for many years to come.

It will be necessary to call *all* Powers together, and not the belligerents only, because, in the first place, this would ensure the adhesion of them all to the Union of Europe, sothat none of them could, later on, shirk its duty, which would be active intervention whenever a State breaks the peace of the world. Secondly, the Neutrals would be able to plead whatever extenuating circumstances may be put forward on behalf of the aggressors, especially because it may be taken for granted that the Teutonic nations will in the long run have to adopt some other form of Government, with which negotiations could be opened.

We may, after the repeated statements made by the leading politicians of the Great Powers, take it for granted, that there will not be much cession of territory, except in so far, as the principle that nationality will play a decisive role in the shaping of future States in Europe, will be accepted, and that in doubtful cases option will be allowed, possibly by plebiscite. It is futile, at present, to speculate as to possibilities in this respect, but we may at once make ourselves familiar with the principle that Poland and Finland will obtain autonomy in some shape or form, as already stated; that the future of Alsace Lorraine should be decided by the population of those provinces themselves, whose desires and inclinations alone can guide the decisions of the Congress, and that, wherever possible, a generous measure of local self-government will be one of the guiding principles of the Congress.

As to Belgium, she will have to be indemnified in every conceivable manner. For every picture, for every book stolen or destroyed at Louvain and in the other unfortunate cities of that fair land, a picture or a book will have to be supplied from German collections.

CHAPTER XXI.

THE INTERNATIONAL ARMY.

I. The ideal solution of the problem.

It cannot be our purpose here to go into any detailed speculations with regard to future developments of International Law. That law will be gradually evolved by circumstances, and it will be respected *as soon as international relations have the moral background which the Union of Europe alone can afford.* But the States forming it, must, in modern parlance, have the controlling interest in the Union. It must hold *all* the shares. It will be only a "holding Company", but it will thereby have the supreme management. It can only exercise that management by controlling the *International Army.*

We may assume — allowing for differences which do not affect the principle involved — that the population of Europe is as follows:

Russia	115.000.000	inhabitants.
Germany	65.000.000	"
Austria Hungary	50.000.000	"
United Kingdom	42.000.000	"

France	39.000.000	inhabitants.
Italy	34.000.000	"
Spain	19.000.000	"
Belgium	7.500.000	"
Holland	6.500.000	"
Roumania	6.000.000	"
Portugal	6.000.000	"
Switzerland	3.000.000	"
Scandinavia	8.000.000	"
Balkan States & Greece ..	12.000.000	"
Total about	415.000.000	inhabitants.

and one percent of this number, say 4.150.000 men will constitute the International Army whose task will be to protect Europe and to carry out the decrees of International Parliament.

This Army will have to be above all things a military organisation, which, under all circumstances, will be able to enforce the will of Europe, without the least chance of being opposed. Europe will have to remain in a position to defend herself against all possible attacks from outside.

It will absorb a maximum of those individuals who have made the army their career, and who, if all armies are to be brought back to far smaller proportions than at present, would form a class of malcontents and unemployed, and who, generally, would be a great deal in the way. They will be provided for, to start with. The populace, fond of the exciting spectacle, in their monotonous daily life, of bands and soldiers marching past, with plenty of plumes and feathers and glittering buttons and prancing horses, will be pleased as of yore. These are points of importance. If we try to place ourselves in the position of men who have made militarism their daily bread, and of all those who are dependant on them, we can well understand that they would not by any means enjoy the prospect of being sent home for good, and of being asked to shift for themselves. The fact is, that militarism, in the whole of Europe, has become an economic factor of great importance, with a degree of intensity which varies with the degree of militarism. Europe, since the days of Napoleon, has been setting up a class of men, worthy men no doubt, who have chosen economic sterility as their calling. They have never produced anything to eat or to wear or to consume or to live in; you cannot, in reason, turn the entire situation upside down without causing a lasting dislocation of social conditions, in letting these large numbers of officers and men loose upon the labour markets.

Apart from all this, the International Army will be a splendid instrument of international education. The soldiers will have to be made acquainted with the countries where they sojourn, they will have to learn foreign languages and literatures, to study artistic and other accomplishments of nations hitherto foreign to them and thus learn to appreciate the merits of other nationalities. Each country should have as few troops of its own nationality as possible, but the greatest possible number of other nationalities. This is absolutely necessary in order to ensure international control. Without a very decided preponderance of the foreign element, this would not be attained.

Principles like those set forth in this book will take a long time to permeate the masses, who will, for a long time, allow their blind instincts to rule over them. But the brutal instincts of large and small States must be driven together, like wild beasts, behind a fence, built by International Law, held by an International Army. *States must defend themselves, and one another, against their own evil passions.*

A civilised man, who is yet a man of flesh and blood, subject to all the lusts and passions which no mortal man can escape, knows how to control them if he wishes to deserve the name of a good citizen of the State; *he keeps the beast within at bay,* for he has fenced it in by the supreme power of his will which knows no master but Moral Law.

I hold, that conglomerates of individuals ought not to bow before any other Moral Law than that which they recognise individually as imperative. And just as within the State Man obeys the laws which he has made so as to protect men against each other and against themselves, he should learn to make and obey laws which States will make, to protect each other and themselves against themselves. In this way alone can we hope that States will be less like blind and deaf natural phenomena, possessing as little notion of morality as an earthquake or a whale.

In order to elucidate the composition of the International Army, as we would propose it, we will take as examples, Holland, as one of the smallest, and Russia as one of the largest of European States and we will assume that in each country the International Army will, as to one quarter part, consist of men of the nationality of that country, the other three quarters being made up of the other nationalities.

For Holland, then, we would arrive at the following numbers:

16.250	Hollanders
13.800	Russians
7.800	Germans.
6.000	Austro-Hungarians
5.040	Britishers.
4.680	French.
4.010	Italians.
2.280	Spaniards.
900	Belgians.
720	Roumanians.
720	Portuguese.
2.800	other nationalities.
Total 65.000	men.

and for Russia:

278.000	Russians.
180.700	Germans.
139.000	Austro-Hungarians.
116.760	Britishers.
108.420	French.
94.520	Italians.
52.820	Spaniards.
20.850	Belgians.
18.070	Hollanders.
16.680	Roumanians.
16.680	Portuguese.
71.750	other nationalities.
Total 1.115.000	men.

In each country, therefore, the national element would be so much in the minority, that not a single nation could oppose the decrees of International Parliament, provided, however, that the International Army, represented by a General Staff in each country, will be the sole armed and organised force (local Police being excepted) and that the manufacturing and the sale of all war-material, and of aircraft will be under its control, and will be regulated by International Law. The Army would not owe obedience to any power except to International Parliament, to which each individual soldier would have to swear allegiance. The quantity of fire-arms and of ammunition to be manufactured annually would have to be fixed for each State, and the possession of fire-arms, except for sporting purposes, should be made punishable and should be only allowed to those who hold a special permit from the General Staff.

When a State wishes to suppress sedition or revolt in its territory, it will have the right to call the Army to its aid. If a State does so more often than International Parliament thinks desirable, such a State cannot, evidently, manage its own affairs and will be placed under International control until self-Government can be allowed.

When a State wishes to annex any foreign territory, it will only be allowed to do so with the sanction of International Parliament. This sanction being once obtained the State may use the entire International Army assigned to it, even reinforced by contingents from neighbouring States. Annexations, however, can never be allowed except on condition that the annexing State will enjoy no commercial privileges from them, conferred by tariffs.

The numerical strength of the Army may by some be considered too great. But it is not instituted exclusively for International Policework. One of its main purposes is the bringing together of various nationalities in friendly co-operation. It would, after a short time, create a wide-spread knowledge, hitherto quite inconceivable, of other lands and folks, in all layers of society; an immense amount of international prejudice would disappear; the knowledge of languages, international intercourse and commerce would increase enormously.

In order to make it impossible for the populace to distinguish nationalities, which would be dangerous in times of riot or of international friction or intrigue, there must be no difference in uniform.

Each batallion of 1000 men should consist as much as possible of a great variety of nationalities, and even in companies this principle should be adopted as much as possible. This is absolutely necessary in order to render conspiracies impossible or easily exposed. Only the small and unaggressive nationalities like the Swiss, Dutch and Scandinavians may be allowed to form entire companies. But after all we have seen of the spirit of German nationality, and of its aggressive fanaticism, German soldiers should be treated with a certain amount of misgiving; and it would probably be desirable not to allow to Germany the same percentage of international soldiers as to the other nationalities, until their feelings can be more fully trusted.

The question regarding the language of command will certainly form a very serious difficulty. We do not believe much in international languages made to order, like Volapük or Esperanto. There is, however, a language which for many centuries has been international: viz. Latin, the use of which would not hurt the national feelings of any country or contingent. It would no doubt be easily adaptable for military command and for official documents. If Latin is considered impracticable, English, Spanish and French would have about equal rights. German, on account of its difficult grammar and the length of the words, like Dutch, would be out of the question. The same, I suppose, would apply to Russian with its intricate grammar. But once the nations of the civilised world could be got so far as to recognise their common interests, the question of language could never stand in the way.

In avoiding too low a limit of age, international marriages and tourism would be much increased. For immeasurably more people than at present this rich and splendid world, which fools have partly transformed into a *Hell*, would be open.

The level of the Army should be kept as high as possible, and the service should be so organised that every man would consider it an honour to be able to enlist, and that parents would look upon serving in the International Army as an excellent "finishing touch" to the education fo their sons. In this way hundreds of thousands will serve without pay and will provide their own outfit. For those who do not possess private means the State will have to provide. Large numbers of the less well educated classes may be enlisted by way of reward for particular merit.

We shall of course have to reckon with the "vested interests" of the military caste, especially in so far as these interests are represented by the nobility. It would certainly be very dangerous to appoint Dukes and Princes and Counts etc. over regiments of their own nationality. We do not for a moment wish to say anything derisive or deprecating about titled persons generally. For all we know, the majority of them may be the best people in the world, and men of the greatest possible merit. From their midst very often the cleverest Statesmen and diplomats are recruited; although I am not certain that the men who are wounded or maimed in the present war will look upon this as a particular merit. But here again, as in the case of large States, the nobility *is there*, and we have to reckon with it, and make the best of it. We have, however, to keep the *mob* within certain limits and we have to protect it against its own inherited propensity to adore Dukes, Princes, etc. who may be their landlords and before whom, poor creatures, they are almost sure to start automatically bowing and shouting patriotic and aggressive phrases in all sorts of languages: German, Russian, Hungarian, Slavonic, Ruthenic etc. It is a well-known saying, in England, that an Englishman "dearly loves a Lord". If that is said of free Britons, what will be the mental attitude of those nations who still recognise feudal rights instead of looking upon them as a forgotten thing of the past? I do not say that feudalism and all that sort of thing is so very despicable. I dare say that in a country where the people, or a part of them, are sufficiently simple-minded or amiable, or stupid, or possess a given mixture of all these qualities together even, nobilities and feudal rights may be quite nice and comfortable. But since, as we think we have proved in the case of Germany, these notions lead or may lead, to organised murder, it is another matter. It will, therefore, be necessary to take measures to prevent undesired developments. This, we think, could be accomplished if the Law were to prohibit commands to be given to titled persons over troops of their own nationality. A Hungarian count, for instance, would be allowed to command a Danish regiment, with all the honours due to him. A Slavonic Baron would be eligible to a command over a Swiss regiment.

Several authors have pleaded the forming of an International Police (1), thinking that armies could be abolished, and that the executive power of International Parliament could be entrusted to one or more Neutral Powers. I think these ideas are fundamentally wrong.

In the first place, as already pointed out, standing armies mean vested interests. One might as well try to abolish the church, or the baker. If serious attempts were made to abolish standing armies there would be a tremendous opposition by the vested interests, which, we may be certain, are very influential and powerful in all countries. Moreover, society likes troops. There is no denying it. When the Emperor or the King or the President opens an exhibition or launches a ship, or receives the Chief of another State, troops must line

(1) Vide *War Obviated by International Police,* Martinus Nijhoff 1915.

the road and present arms, bands must play and reviews must be held. When there is an earthquake or some other catastrophe, troops are required to keep order and to make themselves useful. Your cook likes to spend her sundays with a smart soldier. Young men like the life of a soldier, marching, camping out, riding, fencing etc., and the spirit of order and correctness does them good in more senses than one. If, therefore, we plead the abolishment of standing armies, we must give society a substitute, and an International Army will be far and away the best possible substitute.

Secondly, if one or more Neutral Powers were entrusted with the task of maintaining an International Army, there would be no certainty that some large Power, or a combination of Powers large and small, would not, at a given moment, sweep the International Army away. *International treaties and agreements have not the slightest value* as long as the majority of States do not combine in the way we have sketched.

As long as the interests of civilised States are looked upon as opposed to each other, a combination will be impossible, *and International Law will remain a farce.*

The sooner this is recognised, the better; and those States whose mailed fist is the strongest, will have at least a small chance of escaping the total destruction which threatens Europe after another decade or generation, or within the next century at the very latest.

II. An Alternative Solution.

We are quite ready to admit that the proposition to let the International Army be formed by all the nations of Europe combined, may not be practicable in our time, especially because Germany and her unlimited ambitions will stand in the way, if peace is concluded before the Teutons have been thoroughly vanquished.

We have put the proposition forward, nevertheless, as a matter of principle, because we believe that in writing about International affairs it is imperatively necessary to aim high. It is, certainly, the easiest thing in the world to say that all these propositions are utopian and hyper-idealistic. Any fool can do that. There is not a single achievement among the endless number of human endeavours for the betterment of humanity's fate on this planet which was not, at its inception, ridiculed as utopian. If you hear what cynics say about Internationalism in politics, and about ideas like those set forth in this little book, you will but hear repetitions of phrases of some centuries or generations ago, when the idealists of yore were laughed and ridiculed out of court.

But for those idealists, dear reader, you would at any moment be liable to have some ferocious chieftain's acolytes open your door, lift you from your bed and hang you for not saying your prayers in the way he ordered, or put you to the torture at some malicious enemy's behest. But for those ridiculous idealists, you might still be a serf, walking about with a rope round your neck, always ready for being strung up on the nearest tree by order of your Landlord, for some paltry offense. But for those ridiculous utopians, in short, neither your life, nor your property nor your wife's and children's lives would be safe for a moment.

It is very easy, too, to declare that wars between nations are in the nature of things; that it is no use trying to do away with them, and that War is simply *a fact* one has to put up with. *But the entire History of Civilisation is one continued and determined refusal to put up with facts of that sort.* In the past some very ridiculous idealists and fools declined to be at the mercy of gangs of scoundrels, who called themselves the masters of the land and who could hang anybody they liked. The foolish idealists strung them up by their own ropes and so got rid of them. Other poor fools declined to put up with plague and pestilence and they invented means to wipe them out.

It has been held that in order to abolish war, human nature has to be altered. But would anybody be ready to declare that since torture, slavery and serfdom have been abolished, since religious liberty has been proclaimed, since famine and plague have become obsolete and rare, human nature has changed? One might as well say that Gravitation has changed.

That the ideals of one generation become commonplace realities of the next, is too often overlooked.

Again, there is quite a sufficient number of persons, who, from mental laziness, or from bitterness, or cynicism, or from a combination of all these, declare that it is hopeless to try and improve the world. We may leave them to enjoy whatever anaesthetics they may derive from antiquated religious beliefs, or from a devotion to modern art which has no moral background.

For all that, whilst not losing sight of our ideal solution, it may, for the present, be advisable to turn to the next best way out of the difficulty.

We have, quite recently, seen England and France arranging a combination of financial operations in the money market of the U. S., which is, like everything else in this war, without precedent. We have witnessed England granting financial support to her Allies in a way which suggests the closest and most intimate International relations that can be imagined. We are, daily, recording the most remarkable co-operation of heterogeneous military forces of all time, when we record the battles fought by the Allies to carry out one great strategical aim. We are, in fact, witnessing, under our very eyes, (1) the formation of that very International Army, which hitherto only existed in the

(1) In this case we have to record a gradual development from the complicated to the simple, from diversity to unity, *in the face of common danger*. In Holland, when the dykes break, even the most quarrelsome neighbours co-operate in repairing them. They are *brothers* even though they cordially detest each other. They *have got to recognize* the Brotherhood of Man, if they would avoid ruin.

phantastic dreams of idealists like the Abbé de St. Pierre, who, already in the 18th Century, advocated it.

The International Army is there. Will it be possible for the nations whose armies at present constitute that Force, to evolve a permanent combination, and to persuade several other states to join them?

The principle of *mutual territorial occupation*, to which what is recommended in this essay, really amounts, would indeed do away to a very great extent with that sovereignty, which many authorities have held up as the essential attribute of the State, since only the complete exercise of its authority will ensure its liberty of action.

But is that very liberty of action, which has been praised up to the skies, indeed such a priceless treasure as they would have us believe?

The History of Civilisation constitutes an unbroken record of a series of restrictions of individual liberty of action. Only such barbarous and declining wild tribes as those of New Guinea do not know of any restrictions to their individual liberty to murder and rob their neighbours, of no restrictions to the exercise of their vile passions. That is why they are bound to disappear.

It cannot be admitted that States should adhere to a Moral Code, to which honest individuals could not subscribe. That Code, in reality, is made up of a variety of restrictions of individual liberty. Since Man, if he would at all survive as a species, has been forced to think out a Moral Code for himself, it is utterly unthinkable that agglomerates of individuals, called States, could ignore that Code, without compassing their own destruction.

We are, indeed, witnessing the commencement of Europe's self-destruction, which Germany has started by invading her neighbours and by destroying some parts of Europe. It is useless to close our eyes to it. *The work of the destruction of European civilisation has begun.* And here we have the result of the exercise of that liberty of action, of that State-sovereignty, which is claimed as the essential attribute of the State.

Evidently, then, that sovereignty is highly undesirable, if European civilisation is to be saved at all.

Unfortunately war is viewed differently by the different nations of the world. Germany and Austria proclaim war as a thing to be desired. The Balkan races appear to thrive on mutual slaughter. The Turks have scarcely ever done anything well except fighting. But the Anglo-Saxons of Great Britain and of her Sister-States in America and elsewhere never cease proclaiming their utmost abhorrence of war, which they call dirty work. France and Russia probably hold the same view. At all events they do not, in their literature, possess any proof to the contrary. In this they differ from the Teutons, whose literature abounds in panegyrics of warlike actions and bloody deeds. The Governments of France and Russia have proclaimed their love of peace on all possible occasions, whilst Russia instigated the first Peace Conference. Moreover, Great Britain, Russia, France, and the United States have satiated their land-hunger. It is pretty much the same with Italy.

When the present war is over, all belligerent powers will have lost hundreds of thousands of men, whose intellectual force would have been indispensable for the management and development of fresh territories. It cannot, therefore, be supposed, that for some generations to come, they will go to war, except in self-defence.

If, then, those Powers, who at present form the International Police, are sincere in their desire to abolish war, there is but one course open to them: *they must make it impossible, for other Powers, after the wàr, to separate them.* That they are sincere in their desire to abolish war is nothing but a truism; although it should never be forgotten, that about ninety out of a hundred persons have never seen war at all, and have not the faintest conception of its horror, of its misery and of its wickedness. For many of them the old lies about glory, the old buncombe about military courage and all the rest of it will remain things which will stir them up as soon as they hear the drum or the bugle, or behold the gold-lace that is meant to blind their eyes to the bloody significance of national armies.

But to separate them will be the most fervent desire of the Teutonic Powers. The German papers, with evident satisfaction, recently reported a statesman to have declared that the nations, who now fight side by side, *may well be opponents in the next conflict.* We know that no treaty or agreement whatsoever can avert conflicts, as long as there is no International Army to keep order. It should certainly not be assumed, for a moment, that Germany and Austria, whatever the outcome of the present war may be, will be satisfied with isolation in the world.

It is quite true, that ever since the battles of the Aisne and the Yser a victorious Germany, which would be the paramount power in Europe, is unthinkable. Next to being completely vanquished, the best the Teutons may hope for, is a compromise. But even this, as long as public opinion in France and in England and Russia remains what it is, appears only possible as a result of a financial and economic *débacle* in the British Empire and the Allied countries. However, we *may* have to assume that Germany and Austria will remain Great Powers, either combined on separately. This will mean a standing threat to Europe and to Civilisation.

We would, therefore, suggest, that Great Britain, the British Dominions, France, Russia and Italy, now that they have solemnly declared that they will not conclude a separate peace with Germany and her Allies, should go a step further. They should, as a matter of principle, agree to mutual territorial occupation after the war. They should at once inform all the Powers who up to now have remained neutral, that such is their intention, and that Europe, policed by an International Army, and the Oceans by an International Fleet, are what they are fighting for. (1)

As long as they remain in the present stage of vague promises regarding the "rights of small nations" and the "destruction of Prussian militarism", they will not convince the Neutrals that this war is essentially different from previous ones; that it is more than an old-fashioned war, to be followed by an old-fashioned peace. Their glowing passion for "liberty, right and justice", their red-hot indignation at Germany's callous brutality and cynicism will not be of the slightest avail. The Neutrals will continue to feel boundless pity for the victims of the Teutonic conspiracy. But beyond that they will have no reason to help, unless they are forced into war, for help to others may mean self-destruction. *Ultra posse nemo obligatur.* They will continue taking an interest in the situation only in so far as their own selfish interests, in their narrowest national sense, are concerned. The international situation, for them, when the war is over, will open no new prospects of anything better than before. What is said about the rights of small nations, the destruction of Prussian militarism, they will call *words*. The small

(1) We may here quote the following from Sir Edward Grey's communication of the 25th August 1915 to the British Press: „If, in future, we are to have guarantees against wars, they will have to be reasonable, clear and practicable, and to engage Germany as well as other nations, ourselves included".

Neutrals will, as far as the destruction of Prussian militarism is concerned, be glad to eat their cake and have it. But they will remain inactive as long as possible, and they will only think of self-defence. For a divided Europe, after the war, will mean as much danger to them as before it or during it.

But if the Neutrals were confronted with a clear, distinct aim, held up to them by the Entente: a solemn promise of a new, United Europe, their attitude would change. But it would change only, if, beyond the words, they could discern a solid fact, a tangible reality. What the foundations of a newly united Europe might be, we have endeavoured to show in this essay.

If the United States, Spain, Roumania, Sweden and Norway, upon the reception of such a proposal, made to them each simultaneously by the Entente Powers, were to declare to Germany and to her Allies, that unless they agreed to the proposal for a United Europe, these five States would, one and all, decline any further direct intercourse during the war, the Central Powers would at last know that their cause is hopeless, and they would, if the process of attrition had gone far enough, welcome the Union of Europe as the only way out of the *impasse* into which their aggressiveness has brought them.

Many German authors point to Russia as a constant and invincible menace to their country. But the Russian character, on the whole, is far more peacefully inclined than that of the Potsdam philosophers. Russia will stop being a menace to Germany as soon as Germany recognises Russia as her friend and partner in the work of civilising Europe. Obviously, the Central Powers have the greatest possible interest in a united Europe, as proved by their constant allusions to the "Russian danger".

Holland and Denmark may find it impossible to go so far as to threaten a suspension of relations. But the other Powers would incur no great risk in so doing, and they could very well avail themselves of the international organisation which exists at the Hague, carrying on relations only through the intermedium of the Court of Arbitration.

If the five remaining Powers: The United States, (1) Spain, Roumania, Sweden, and Norway were to decline any other intercourse, even as a result of the above-named proposal of the Entente, this would not mean a *casus belli*. Firstly, there would be no precedent. And to propose to Germany to carry on diplomatic relations only through the International Court of Arbitration could not possibly be construed by that Power as an unfriendly act.

But it would show Germany the only way to salvation.

---

(1) And, possibly the great South American Republics.

CHAPTER XXII.

NEUTRAL HOLLAND.

Many things which are said in this little volume have no doubt been said before, or thought before, by others. We are all children of our time, and whether we will or not, our acts and our thoughts have to move along with it. They are like the warp, ceaselessly moving on the endless woof of time. But through the varied pattern which relentless History weaves, runs one distinct line, which is always visible. It has the colour of blood, human blood, spilt for the Great Cause of Mankind.

The manhood of the Allies is sacrificing itself in the service of that Cause.

Citizens of neutral countries, like the present author, hold their breath in respect and awe.

The attitude and position of Holland, my native country, I have tried to define in the following article, which I contributed to one of the large daily papers in London last June:

> When the present Liberal Ministry came to power in Holland barely three years ago, after the defeat of the Calvinistic-Roman Catholic Coalition, neither they nor the nation expected that the task entristed to them would, in 1914, assume the weight of an almost crushing responsibility.

They had, indeed, continued the time-honoured traditions of Dutch foreign policy which, for generations, had guided it, quite irrespective of the political party which happened to be in the majority. Those traditions included: whilst keeping the country, strategically speaking, in as good a state of defence against invasion as was compatible with sound finance and with the innate aversion of the Hollanders against militarism, the Ministry of Foreign Affairs was to avoid all causes of friction abroad, to surround itself by as high a wall of mystery as Parliamentary government allowed, and, above all, to avoid joining any of the Great Powers, or their coalitions, irrespective of whether they called themselves alliances or otherwise.

This policy, carried through for generations, had inspired so much confidence, that M. de Beaufort, when he was Minister for Foreign Affairs, succeeded in obtaining for The Hague the honour of being the seat of the first Peace Conference of 1899, which led to that of 1907, and to the establishment of the International Court of Arbitration; and thus The Hague gradually became a very important centre of diplomacy.

THE PERIOD OF SECURITY.

Whilst in the Seventeenth and Eighteenth Centuries Holland had played a *role* in the world which was out of all proportion to its size or population, and which ultimately landed her in the disasters of the days of Napoleon, from which it took her three full generations to recover, Holland, in the Nineteenth and present centuries, had to be, and, indeed, was, quite satisfied with a position to which the device „*ne trop hault, ne trop bas*" would be truly applicable. To have grasped the broad fact that great aspirations would as surely lead to disaster as before, and that no alliance could possibly shield the country against aggression from the opposite camp, is the merit of the level-headed and clear-headed men who guided the destinies of their country ever since 1830.

From that time until long after the Franco-German War, indeed, Holland's position in Europe did not appear to be fraught with any serious difficulties, for although Prussian ambitions may occasionally have caused a certain anxiety, it was by no means clear that Holland could be at all a desirable object for German conquest, for it was perfectly well known in Berlin that the sturdy Dutch race would never submit even to force of arms. As long as Bismarck reigned, there was not the remotest necessity for any German designs against Holland. The game was not worth the candle. The Dutch colonies could never be held by Germany as long as she had no navy. Holland itself afforded no room for Germany's surplus population. But when the words "Germany's future is on the water" were spoken, all this suddenly changed. For from that moment Holland's geographical position, between the Power which was supreme upon the waves and the Power which aspired to that supremacy, became one of extreme peril.

NATIONAL PRECAUTIONS.

Great strength of character, we presume, was needed in the first thirteen years of the Twentieth Century for resisting pressure from either side. The fact that Holland's eastern and southern provinces are open to attack, and cannot be defended, except for a few days, against the strong armies that would invade them in case war; that her western shores and provinces could be threatened from the sea, whilst her vast Eastern Empire would be at the mercy of the Power which ruled the oceans, might well cause even the stoutest heart to tremble. There was but one possible course, and it was taken. The old traditions as to foreign policy were maintained. But the power of resisting invasion was increased enormously. The Army Estimates were increased; the old system of recruiting, under which service in the Army was not compulsory for those who could afford the financial sacrifice needed for providing a substitute was abolished, and compulsory conscript service was placed in its stead; the various lines of defence were constantly improved, the necessity of possessing the best artillery that money could buy was fully taken into account. Moreover, the officers of the Dutch Army had ample time and opportunity for studying Army organisation in Prussia just over the border, and we may take it for granted that they availed themselves of both.

When Germany pressed for the fortification of Flushing and another country opposed it, great care was taken that Holland's decision could not possibly be construed as a desire to join either side. When M. Baie, a distinguished Belgian gentleman, some years anterior to the war, made propaganda for a closer union between Belgium and Holland, his proposals were received with much approval, but officially no steps were taken. The Hollanders preferred to „leave well alone." It is fortunate that they did so, for if the two small Kingdoms had become allies, not Belgium alone, but Holland as well might have been drawn into the war, and last October the Belgian refugees would have had little chance of escape, for the provinces of Noord-Brabant and the southern part of Zeeland, which border on Belgium, could not be successfully defended against invasion, and would have been in German hands.

THE ULTIMATE DEFENCES.

And here we touch upon the extreme difficulty of defending the greater, although not the most important, part of Holland against invasion by land. About two-thirds of the Dutch landfrontiers run along German territory for a distance of over 300 miles. It would be quite hopeless to try and hold such a frontier against Armies counting millions of men. It was fully recognised that Holland could resist invasion of all the eastern and southern provinces for a few short weeks at the most, in order to give the Army time to retire upon the strategical river defences which can effectively shield Holland proper (where the largest and most important cities are situated), and ultimately Amsterdam. These lines consist partly (on the south) of broad and deep rivers, and partly (on the east) of lowlands, easily inundated. In fact, they saved the country in the „frightful year" 1672, when little Holland was attacked simultaneously by England, France, Munster, and Cologne, and when the outlying provinces were partly devastated by French troops and Groningen was besieged by the Germans. What was achieved in 1672, it was claimed, and is still claimed, could be done in our time, and indeed will be done if courage and determination still count for anything. That neither of these qualities is lacking, was proved by the mobilisation of last August, when of all countries Holland mobilised first, and within forty-eight hours 200,000 men were at their appointed posts. We think it will be admitted that this is no small achievement for a country of which the population is less than that of London. And, what is more, an ardent wish for still greater security is being vented in countless newspaper articles and pamphlets, urging further extension of the Army. A few weeks ago a petition to that effect signed by many of the most prominent Hollanders was handed over to the States General and universally and enthusiastically supported.

There cannot be the remotest doubt in the minds of the Dutch nation as to the side from which the danger may come. A more or less friendly feeling which existed before the war has given place to suspicion which the events of the last ten months have created. Hollanders, like Britishers, are fond of quoting Scripture. And in these days the words of St. Matthew, "Be ye therefore wise as serpents and harmless as doves," often come to their minds. But the Dutch dove, if it were compelled to defend itself, would not be a gentle bird by any means.

I believe that what was said in this article, still holds good today, but I should like to add a few remarks regarding the History of our country.

There are three dates in Holland's History, which have been decisive. They occur at intervals of almost exactly a century. They are: 1588, 1688 and 1795.

In 1588 England and Holland joined hands to break the power of a tyrant who would subjugate Europe: Philip of Spain. His soldiers had ravaged the Netherlands. Instead of with fruit, the trees in the orchards were bowed down with the bodies of poor folks who had been hanged by the tyrant's myrmidons. (Hooft-Ned. Hist.) The people of Antwerp fled to Holland in the 16th century to excape murder, as their descendants did in 1914. Fair Flanders groaned under the load of war, as it does today. Then, as now, with the freedom of the Netherlands Britain's liberty stood or fell. Queen Elisabeth knew, and Engeland knew. Philip swore that he would have her blood. Sixtus V excommunicated the Queen, and had de declaration read in the famous Antwerp cathedral. „Words, words words" said Parma, who made a great show of peace-negotiations. „Parma therewith sent many English asleep, and also some pacifists in the Netherlands, not thinking of peace in the least, but only of how to conquer England," says an historian of those days [1]). But the Queen was warned in time. So were the Estates at the Hague and the Stadholder. The Armada was destroyed, partly by Anglo-Dutch co-operation, and partly by the storms which drove it ashore on the coasts of Scotland and Ireland. The Tirpitz of 1588 had done his worst, and failed. Europe could breathe again.

In the 17th Century England and Holland fought, what in England are called „The Dutch wars," and what we in Holland call „The English wars." They were fair fights, between opponents of about equal strength, and both retired from them with honour. There was comparatively little resentment over them,

[1]) „Parma wieghde eensdeels veel Engelsche in slape, ende oock eenighe pays-wenschers in de Nederlanden, nerghens minder dan op vrede te maken denckende, maer gheheel om Engelant te conquesteeren".

for they ruined neither belligerent. Moreover, dynastic ties were very strong in those days. As early as the Middle Ages not less than five Counts of Holland had married Scotch and English Princesses [1]. But in the 17th and 18th centuries three Stadholders in succession, William II, William III, and William IV, followed their example.

In 1688 the Stadholder William III, whose aim in life was the furtherance of Protestantism, and the saving of Europe from the tiranny of Louis XIV, became King of England. This meant that the fate of Holland was linked to that of Great Britain. Some historians declare that William sacrificed Holland's interests to the common cause. But is is impossible to deny that during the reign of the three Stadholders, and especially during that of William III, Holland was very influential in the councils of Europe. Even in the time of William IV, when the Dutch Army and Navy had been allowed to fall into decay, Holland still retained her prominent position.

It is equally impossible to deny that Holland's greatness ended with the last Stadholder, William V, who, did not marry an English Princess, but a niece of Frederick the Great.

---

[1]

Floris I,	about 1160	married	Ada,	daughter of the	King of Scotland;
William I,	„ 1215	„	Mary.	„ „ „	Duke ol Lancaster;
John I,	„ 1295	„	Elisabeth	„ „ „	King of England;
William V	„ 1320	„	Matilde	„ „ „	Duke of Lancaster;
Charles the Bold	± 1350	„	Margaret	„ „ „	Duke of York.

I merely mention historic facts; I draw no conclusions. The reader may draw his own.

It would, of course, be absurd to say that the expression „*travailler pour le roi de Prusse*" dates from that time. William V was incapable and the Dutch democrats wanted to get rid of him. But here the King of Prussia, like a true Prussian, stepped in on the side of absolutism. He sent an army into Holland, and the Stadholder was re-instated. Then came a long string of disasters. That was certainly not the fault of the King of Prussia. He had been supported by England in his intervention in the Stadholder's favour. The fact is that Holland was absolutely at the mercy of the Great Powers.

In 1795, the third of the three important dates, Holland threw in her lot with France, the country against which the European coalition, headed by England, was directed. For France aspired at military preponderance in Europe. Holland, when it was too late, saw that she had „put her money on the wrong horse." But the end was that Holland was made to fight the coalition and was ruined.

The centenary of independance, celebrated in 1913, served as a timely reminder of the misery of those disastrous years, which was not lost on Holland.

By her geographical situation Holland has, for ages, been influenced by the three large neighbouring nations: England, France and Germany. It is difficult to say whose influence she has undergone most. But it is quite certain that she has always been averse to militarism, and that parliamentary government did not come to her from Prussia. In the *Reichstag* only the other day (early in April 1916) Vice-President Paassche declared, as if to remind those who had forgotten, that the *Reichstag* had no voice in any changes in the appointment of Secretaries of State. They were appointed by the Emperor alone. Here we have absolutism pure and simple; a declaration, by the Vice-President himself, that the *Reichstag*, whatever else it may be, is not a parliament in the Western sense of the word.

Owing, chiefly, to the violation of Belgium, the majority in Holland is anti-German. There are many pro-French and many pro-English specialists. The Dutch are often exhorted to be „pro-Dutch" only. But I believe that we can „go one better," in being pro-civilisation.

If Holland is not forced into the war, it may be that, afterwards, she will be expected to reconcile where reconciliation is desired and feasible. It is to be hoped that Germany will not render such a task impossible.

GPSR Compliance

The European Union's (EU) General Product Safety Regulation (GPSR) is a set of rules that requires consumer products to be safe and our obligations to ensure this.

If you have any concerns about our products, you can contact us on ProductSafety@springernature.com

In case Publisher is established outside the EU, the EU authorized representative is:

Springer Nature Customer Service Center GmbH
Europaplatz 3
69115 Heidelberg, Germany

Batch number: 10830935

Printed by Printforce, the Netherlands